**At Issue**

Satanism

# Other Books in the At Issue series:

Antidepressants

Are Conspiracy Theories Valid?

Are Privacy Rights Being Violated?

Child Labor and Sweatshops

Child Sexual Abuse

Creationism Versus Evolution

Does Advertising Promote Substance Abuse?

Does Outsourcing Harm America?

Does the World Hate the United States?

Do Nuclear Weapons Pose a Serious Threat?

Drug Testing

The Ethics of Capital Punishment

The Ethics of Genetic Engineering

The Ethics of Human Cloning

Gay and Lesbian Families

Gay Marriage

Gene Therapy

How Can Domestic Violence Be Prevented?

How Does Religion Influence Politics?

Hurricane Katrina

Is American Society Too Materialistic?

Is Poverty a Serious Threat?

Is the Mafia Still a Force in America?

Legalizing Drugs

Responding to the AIDS Epidemic

Steroids

What Causes Addiction?

# At Issue

# | Satanism

*Allen Gaborro, Book Editor*

**GREENHAVEN PRESS**
*An imprint of Thomson Gale, a part of The Thomson Corporation*

Detroit • New York • San Francisco • New Haven, Conn. • Waterville, Maine • London

GALE

™

Christine Nasso, *Publisher*
Elizabeth Des Chenes, *Managing Editor*

© 2007 Thomson Gale, a part of The Thomson Corporation.

Thomson and Star logo are trademarks and Gale and Greenhaven Press are registered
trademarks used herein under license.

*For more information, contact:*
Greenhaven Press
27500 Drake Rd.
Farmington Hills, MI 48331-3535
Or you can visit our Internet site at http://www.gale.com

**ALL RIGHTS RESERVED**
No part of this work covered by the copyright hereon may be reproduced or used in any
form or by any means—graphic, electronic, or mechanical, including photocopying, recording, taping, Web distribution, or information storage retrieval systems—without the written
permission of the publisher.

Articles in Greenhaven Press anthologies are often edited for length to meet page require-
ments. In addition, original titles of these works are changed to clearly present the main
thesis and to explicitly indicate the author's opinion. Every effort is made to ensure that
Greenhaven Press accurately reflects the original intent of the authors. Every effort has
been made to trace the owners of copyrighted material.

Cover photograph reproduced by permission of Corbis RM, Metaphotos.

---

**LIBRARY OF CONGRESS CATALOGING-IN-PUBLICATION DATA**

Satanism / Allen Gaborro, book editor.
   p. cm. -- (At issue)
  Includes bibliographical references and index.
  ISBN-13: 978-0-7377-2414-1 (lib. : alk. paper)
  ISBN-10: 0-7377-2414-5 (lib. : alk. paper)
  ISBN-13: 978-0-7377-2415-8 (pbk. : alk. paper)
  ISBN-10: 0-7377-2415-3 (pbk. : alk. paper)
  1. Satanism. I. Gaborro, Allen.
  BL480.S38 2006
  133.4'22--dc22

                      2006026964

---

Printed in the United States of America
10 9 8 7 6 5 4 3 2 1

# Contents

Introduction     **7**

1. The Prevalence of Satanism Is Exaggerated     **10**
   *Joe Abrams*

2. The Satanic Underground Is Real and Growing     **18**
   *Jen Shroder*

3. Satanism Is Linked to Multiple Crimes     **22**
   *Thomas D. Elias*

4. Reports of Satanic Crimes Are Not Credible     **27**
   *Cecil E. Greek*

5. Satanism Promotes a Culture of Death     **35**
   *Jim Howell*

6. Satanists Say Their Religion Is Misunderstood     **39**
   *Ed Power*

7. Satanism Promotes Ritual Violence     **44**
   *Harun Yahya*

8. Satanists Use Violence Only for Self-Defense     **50**
   *Vexen Crabtree*

9. The Negative Aspects of Satanism Outweigh the Positives     **60**
   *D. Rebecca Deinsen*

10. Counselors Can Help Students Reject Satanic Cults     **67**
    *Lee J. Richmond*

11. The Psychology Behind Beliefs About Satanism Is Deluded     **72**
    *Malcolm McGrath*

Organizations to Contact     **77**

Bibliography     **81**

Index     **87**

# Introduction

Although Satanism has existed in various forms for nearly as long as Christianity itself, contemporary Satanism is most often associated with Anton LaVey, who established the Church of Satan in the mid-1960s. The institution was the first organized satanic church in the world. The Church of Satan, a product of the counterculture movement of the period, promoted indulgence over moderation, revenge rather than "turning the other cheek," and vitality over weakness. Other tenets of LaVey's creed, known as the Nine Satanic Statements, justified violence in some situations and placed value on what he called pure knowledge over so-called self-hypocrisy. LaVey's philosophy both attracted strict adherents and inspired a multiplicity of other interpretations of satanism. As a result, modern-day satanism came to encompass various branches and philosophies.

Whatever its form, satanism gained little widespread notice until the 1980s, when fears over the perceived threat of satanism swept the United States. Much of this anxiety resulted from the publication of the book *Michelle Remembers* in 1980. The book recounts the story of a young female child's supposed personal exposure to horrifying satanic rituals. In his book *Demons of the Modern World*, researcher Malcolm McGrath writes that *Michelle Remembers* went on to "become the bible of the Satanism scare."

*Michelle Remembers* convinced many people that satanism was a real danger. The book helped create the impression that there was a vast, underground satanic conspiracy, and that covert Satanic cults existed across the country from the smallest towns to the biggest cities. This impression was fueled by the media: Talk shows featured guests who said they had witnessed satanic rituals like those described in *Michelle Remem-*

*bers*, and news outlets reported on individual murderers who claimed their crimes were motivated by satanism.

The most pervasive accounts of criminal acts linked to satanism during this period were of what became known as satanic ritual abuse (SRA). SRA refers to a number of activities, including suspected brainwashing and maltreatment of individuals. More disturbing were reports of children being sexually abused on an enormous scale by a satanic network. There were also stories of satanic-based ritualized murders and the abduction of children for human sacrifice. Some people went so far as to claim that Satanists bred human babies solely for the purpose of sacrificing them.

Evidence to support these allegations, however, was frequently lacking. In time, even investigators who initially believed the reports concluded that they were false and that supposedly satanic crimes were most often committed by dabblers in satanism who were unconnected to any larger organization. Today, most experts believe that *Michelle Remembers* is a fraud, and fears of an extensive satanic underground have largely faded.

Yet there are those who continue to argue that the satanism of bloody rituals, child abductions, sadistic murders, and human sacrifices does exist and remains a threat, particularly to adolescents. Teens, they say, are especially susceptible to satanic beliefs because so many feel lonely and alienated from society. Satanism gives these disaffected youths a sense of security and acceptance into a welcoming community. In exchange, however, opponents warn, these youths are expected to perform ritual violence as a form of tribute to Satan.

But as forceful as detractors are in their allegations against satanism, its devotees are equally emphatic in defending their faith against social condemnation. Satanists categorically deny that satanism encourages human sacrifices or the harming of innocents. They regard such accusations as nothing but embroidered urban legends that are light-years from the truth and are intended to produce an unfounded hysteria against satanism. Criminals who cite satanic involvement as the reason for their crimes, they say, do not truly understand what real satanism is.

Satanists state that far from being a destructive force, satanism is a life-affirming belief system that espouses a will to freedom in response to the demands of the modern world. They also claim that it draws on the strength of the individual self and its desire to stand out among the crowd of mass society. Adherents also say satanism teaches integrity, independence, nonconformity, and self-confidence. On the subject of violence, satanists in general stress that they are appalled by arbitrary acts of aggression. Violence of any kind is permissible only in cases of warranted revenge or in instances in which self-preservation is at stake.

This polarity of views means that it is nearly impossible to objectively answer the question of whether satanism is at its core a belief system based on immorality and criminality or the victim of distortion by misguided groups and individuals. Efforts to reach any kind of consensus on the essence of satanism have most often failed. Whatever the case may be, it is a sure bet that the truth about satanism will always be the subject of endless contention and debate.

# 1

# The Prevalence of Satanism Is Exaggerated

*Joe Abrams*

*Joe Abrams is a former sociology of religion student at the University of Virginia. He has written several articles on satanism.*

*Satanist groups cannot be easily categorized by a single set of beliefs. Yet a series of satanic panics occurred in American society during the 1980s, during which claims were made of a large, well-organized, nationwide satanic conspiracy. Despite such claims, no credible evidence has ever been found to prove that such an underground movement exists. Even claims by people who say they remember suffering abuse from Satanists are questionable. Still, myths about an underground satanic movement persist as a result of popular culture's fascination with Satanism.*

Many people use the term "Satanism" to refer to very different religions and practices. In America, some evangelical and fundamentalist Christian organizations have used the term to define as "Satanic" any practice other than their own particular versions of Christianity. A more common cultural definition includes any religious practice that some consider part of the occult, including Wicca, Vodun, Santeria, and other Neopagan traditions. All of these, however, have completely different beliefs, practices, and social structures, and none of them are "Satanic." In order to better understand the term "Satanism," one must first examine the roots of the word.

Joe Abrams, "Satanism: An Introduction," Religious Movements Homepage Project, University of Virginia, 2000, revised by Kelly Wyman, 2006. http://religiousmovements .lib.virginia.edu/nrms/satanism/intro.html. Reproduced by permission of the author.

*The Oxford English Dictionary* offers three definitions of the word "Satanism":

> 1. A Satanic or diabolical disposition, doctrine, spirit, or contrivance. 2. The characteristics of the 'Satanic school.' 3. The worship of Satan, alleged to have been practised in France in the latter part of the 19th century; the principles and rites of the Satanists.

This first definition originated from *An Apologie of the Church of England* written by Thomas Harding (1565). During the 16th century, the word "Satanism" referred to both Protestants and Catholics, depending on which Christian group was using the term. The second definition refers to any writings or teachings of authors and poets such as Lord Byron. And, the third definition refers to the actual worship of Satan as a god. For a more detailed look at these three definitions, and a discussion of 19th-century "Satanism," see Gareth J. Medway, *Lure of the Sinister: The Unnatural History of Satanism* (2001).

While these definitions are useful in understanding the roots of the word "Satanism," none provide solid characteristics of what Satanism actually incorporates. As well, none of them explain modern Satanic practices such as those of the Church of Satan or the Temple of Set. . . . The following is offered as a working definition of modern Satanism.

## Modern Satanism

Most modern Satanists are atheistic. They do not believe in or worship any specific deity, Satan or otherwise. Instead, they honor what they consider the spirit of Satan. Modern Satanists tend to follow what they believe are the ideals of Satan, and present him as an ideal whose traits are to be emulated. Satan is often represented as a symbol of resistance to dominant religious traditions (e.g., Christian, Jewish, Buddhist, Hindu). Some examples of organizations that follow this practice are the Church of Satan, the First Church of Satan, and the Temple of Set. This form of Satanism is generally referred to as "philosophical Satanism."

While they are in the minority, some modern Satanists are theistic. They believe in Satan as a real entity. The Order of Nine Angels, for example, believes that Satan, as well as other "dark forces," are individual entities beyond human control. Members of this group strive to become "one" with these sinister beings, and seek "to create new, more highly evolved individuals" through the practice of what they call "traditional Satanism" (Long 1994). This form of Satanism is generally referred to as "religious Satanism."

As with any other religion, there are divisions of belief within modern Satanism, both between different groups and between members of the same group.

## Historical Satanism

Like many other religious traditions, Satanism has a long and involved history. The following is a brief outline of the history and roots of Satanism.

While some groups claim that one of the earliest roots of modern Satanism began with the ancient Egyptian god Set (ca. 3200–700 B.C.E.), historian Jeffrey Burton Russell disagrees. Russell writes that all Egyptian gods were ambivalent, and "there is no etymological connection between Set and Satan". He goes on to explain that "the human concept of Satan was developed in Mazdaism, Judaism, Christianity, and Islam precisely for the purpose of personifying radical evil".

The period from the 15th to the 17th centuries marks the richest history in the development of what is now termed Satanism. In 1486, two Dominican friars, Heinrich Kramer and Jacob Sprenger, wrote the *Malleus Maleficarum*, or *The Hammer of Witches*, which purported to detail the various activities of "Satanic witchcraft." These included such acts as flying on broomsticks, having wild sexual orgies, eating children, and inducing plagues. According to Russell, the idea of diabolical witchcraft originated "under the influence of Aristotelian scholasticism, [when] it was believed that natural magic did not exist and that magic could be effective only through the aid of Lucifer and his minions".

The black arts and various occult practices resurfaced in the late 19th century. In France, it was believed that Freemasons were involved in Satan worship. Satan also became a symbol for the French revolution through writers such as Eliphas Lévi. In 19th-century French culture, Satan was often depicted as a political figure, though whose side he was on changed constantly depending on who made the charges.

In 1875, the Theosophical Society was founded by Madame Helena Blavatsky, and another occult organization, the Hermetic Order of the Golden Dawn, twelve years later. One of the most prominent members in the later years of the Hermetic Order of the Golden Dawn was Aleister Crowley, a name that has come to be synonymous with popular understandings of Satanism in the 20th century. Although Crowley was not technically a Satanist, he did claim to be "the Beast 666" from the book of Revelation, and some of his ideas and practices would later be incorporated into modern Satanism. In 1930s Paris, a Luciferian temple was established by Maria de Naglowska, and it is believed that her organization is still active in France.

---

No solid evidence indicating the presence of an organized Satanic underground has ever been discovered.

---

In 1966, the Church of Satan was created by Anton LaVey, and has become arguably the most well known branch of the Satanic movement. In 1969, LaVey published *The Satanic Bible*. The Order of Nine Angels, a group of theistic Satanists, was also created in the 1960s. The Temple of Set broke away from LaVey's Church of Satan, and in 1975 was granted non-profit church status in California. In 1994, another splinter group, the First Church of Satan, was created by John Allee, a former member of LaVey's group.

While some sources claim that the number of Satanists worldwide numbers in the millions, there are currently no accurate membership numbers available and these estimates are almost certainly high.

## Modern Satanic Panics

The 1980s saw a wave of Satanic panics that spread through America. "Satan mongers," often conservative Christians, alleged that a huge underground Satanic conspiracy was responsible for any number of horrific crimes. Some of these estimated the number of Satanists nationwide in the millions. This Satanic underground, they charge, is responsible for such crimes as torturing and mutilating animals, child pornography and molestation, child kidnappings, and the ritualistic murder of men, women, and children. Indeed, some estimate that there are between fifty thousand and two million children sacrificed to Satan every year.

A number of different people have sought to verify the existence of such Satanic cults. In 1980, Michelle Smith published *Michelle Remembers*, which told gruesome stories of being abused at the hands of an organized Satanic cult. Nearly a decade later, Lauren Stratford gained national attention with her book, *Satan's Underground*, in which she claimed to have been used as a "baby breeder" to provide Satanic cults with sacrificial victims. Through sensationalized Christian ministries such as "Talk Back with Bob Larson," numerous other people have testified that they are personal witnesses to the horrors of Satanism.

This all sounds quite dreadful, but the plain fact is that *no solid evidence indicating the presence of an organized Satanic underground has ever been discovered.* How, then, has all this testimonial evidence surfaced?

## Recovered Memory Therapy Controversy

While some has obviously been simply invented, other so-called evidence can be explained through a process known as Recovered Memory Therapy (RMT). During the 1980s and early 1990s, many therapists used this process in an attempt to unearth memories of abuse that their clients had suffered as children. They assumed that most troubled patients had suffered terrible trauma at a young age, and it was the job of the therapist to uncover the trauma and help them work through it. The problem was that many therapists did not so much discover repressed memories as help their patients co-create them. As a result of suggestive and leading questions, hypnotism, implantation of ideas, and coercive conversation, thousands or even tens of thousands of confused patients "remembered" being abused as children, sometimes by their parents, and often at the hands of Satanic cults. Many families were torn apart as a result of these accusations. During the 1990s, more and more mental health organizations determined that RMT often produced false memories in the minds of patients and warned against the further use of these techniques. Countless patients recanted the memories supposedly gained through RMT, and many therapists were sued for damages caused. Now such practices are widely regarded as hopelessly flawed.

> *The fear of 'satanic cults' is a manifestation of social paranoia in times of uncertainty.*

Much of what the patients had "remembered" had been proven to be either unlikely, impossible, or outright false. Patients gave names that did not exist; they named times when they were "baby breeders" when they were clearly not pregnant. They contradicted themselves frequently, and they accused people of committing crimes they could not possibly have committed.

## Social Paranoia of Satanic Panics

Yet in the 1980s, these methods were widely accepted and panics about Satanic cults flourished. This may have been enhanced by the rise of the Religious Right early in the decade, many of whose members actively promoted the idea. This group tended to characterize as immoral (and thus Satanic) such things as heavy metal music, role-playing games like *Dungeons and Dragons*, increasing violence on TV, in movies, and through other types of popular culture such as videogames.

As sociologist Jeffrey S. Victor puts it, however, studies of "Satanic panics" have found that "the fear of 'satanic cults' is a manifestation of social paranoia in times of uncertainty". Victor found that these panics occurred most often in areas of economic hardship and turmoil, where people were insecure about their ability to provide a regular family life. The rumors of Satanic activities, such as murdering helpless pets or sacrificial victims, were symbolic of their feelings of helplessness. These rumors, especially the ones that feared satanic activities on a given Halloween or Friday the 13th, were never authenticated.

Distortion of evidence, whether willful or accidental, contributed much to these panics. Occasionally a group of pets or livestock would be found mutilated, but most of these cases were found to be caused by wild animals such as wolves or coyotes. Instances would occur where a ghastly crime was committed and accompanied by Satanic symbolism; yet there was no cause for believing these were committed by anyone more than a deranged individual who dabbled in Satanism, but who did not belong to any formal Satanic organization. Where there was even the potential for support for a case of Satanic cult behavior, facts simply became blown out of proportion.

The sheer numerical estimates for a large Satanic underground are clearly incompatible with the almost complete lack of evidence. The claim that tens of thousands of babies are ritually murdered each year has not been supported in any way. No one has been proven to be a "baby breeder" for a Satanic cult. There are not enough children kidnapped to allow for these ritual infanticides. However disturbing, the majority of child kidnappings are simply parents fighting over custody: the number of child kidnappings committed by strangers has been documented at well under 100 per year. Of those, half are recovered within 5 years.

# 2

# The Satanic Underground Is Real and Growing

## Jen Shroder

*Jen Shroder is the founder of Blessed Cause, a nonprofit Christian organization dedicated to social issues.*

*The news media too easily disregards the possible involvement of satanic cults in cases of missing women and children, thousands of which have occurred in California. A prime example is the case of Scott Peterson, who was convicted in 2004 of murdering his wife, Laci, and their unborn son, Connor. News reports about the case ignored the fact that there is a thriving satanic group in the town of Modesto, where the Petersons lived, and that such groups may believe in the cleansing power of sacrificing human infants.*

I don't get it. My favorite columnists are writing volumes to hang Scott Peterson. Crowds at the courthouse are being compared to lynch mobs. Peterson is being compared to Hitler, Ted Bundy, Jeffrey Dahmer and a hit list of gruesome ax murdering child molesters. But the columnists forgot one thing, where's the evidence?

The news media has laughed a little too hard at the possibility of a satanic cult. If you do the research, there are *thousands* of unrecovered missing women and children in California that the media ignores. There *are* childhood survivors of satanic cults who have testified to graphic descriptions of sib-

Jen Shroder, "In Lone Defense of Scott Peterson," Blessed Cause, 2004. www.blessedcause.org/protest/scott%20peterson.htm. Reproduced by permission of the author.

lings being tortured to death. Recently in Italy, two teenage members of a heavy metal rock band called the "Beasts of Satan" were killed by other band members in a human sacrifice involving black candles, goats' skulls and sexual violence. In Houston, Texas, a police officer *gave school children satanic sex calendars* featuring explicit details on satanic and sexual rituals for every day of the month.

In 1988 Geraldo Rivera received heavy criticism and pressure for reporting on Satan's Underground, creating a satanic panic. His reports included butchered infants, breeding of babies for later sacrifice during satanic rituals, ritual sexual abuse of children, mutilation of infants, drinking of blood, dismembered corpses, cannibal cults and sex orgies. There were *"gruesome rituals,"* and *"gruesome memories,"* and *"gruesome allegations,"* and *"brutally violent, horrible crimes,"* and acts *"so incredibly outrageous, so incredibly unbelievable,"* that he was reluctant to describe them. *"The most gruesome scenes are left out,"* said Rivera.

> *"Estimates are that there are over 1 million Satanists in this country.... The majority of them are linked in a highly organized, very secretive network. From small towns to large cities, they have attracted police and FBI attention to their Satanic ritual child abuse, child pornography and grisly Satanic murders. The odds are that this is happening in your town."*

*Ritual killings and abuse go on throughout the country.*

## A Satanic Connection to Murder?

Laci's hometown has a satanic group called "The Order of the Lion" where it was last reported to have 20 to 30 members. Near the time of Laci's kidnapping, a brown van "adorned with satanic symbols" was sighted near the Peterson home and some witnesses "recalled a group of suspicious men, one sporting a 666 tattoo, in the area."

In relation to "The Order of the Lion's" previous crimes, Modesto attorney William Arthur Miller said he recalled a member saying that the "sacrifice of a newborn baby was the 'cleaningest' thing you could do. I took that to mean the most cleansing," Miller said. A review of some of the writings revealed references to altars, witchcraft, blood-letting curses, dining with the dead, pentagrams, demons, goats, visions, secret oaths and "the father of darkness."

On the eastern edge of the San Francisco Bay near where the bodies of Laci and Connor washed up, huge paintings on sheets of plywood depict scenes of fire-breathing devils and ax-wielding grim reapers. One painting shows a man and woman in a canoe, with what appears to be three floating babies nearby, intertwined with an umbilical cord.

San Diego therapist Mary Battles said she remains convinced that ritual killings and abuse go on throughout the country. "Where you'll find the evidence is in the men and women who went through it and have scars on their bodies," said Battles. She said she has treated 50 people who were victims of satanic cults and, "I still get a steady stream of them."

## Satanism's Fascination with Children

Anyone who has studied satanism knows there is a fascination with the innocence of infants. I knew a woman who witnessed her younger brother dangling from his feet being tortured to death. She was in long-term therapy and had a difficult time dealing with life after growing up in a Satanist family. San Francisco, where Laci and Conner washed up, has an exploding populace of Satanists and is the founding home of the Church of Satan.

Missing and abducted women and children are far more prevalent than realized. According to 2003 government statistics, in California alone, 10,684 adults have gone missing, never recovered. Another 346 missing are ominously listed as "deceased." 4,815 children have gone missing under "Unknown

Circumstances"—when circumstances surrounding the disappearance are unknown. 545 children disappeared under suspicious circumstances that may indicate a stranger abduction, and in 51 cases the stranger abduction was witnessed. Nationwide 58,200 children were abducted by nonfamily members.

Scott Peterson is clearly a first-class heel but I believe the witch-hunt upon him is exactly that, a lynch-mob inspired by witches out to avert the attention on the growing Satanist population and the rituals that *do* happen.

# Satanism Is Linked to Multiple Crimes

*Thomas D. Elias*

*Thomas D. Elias served as the West Coast correspondent for the Scripps Howard News Service until 1995. He now writes a syndicated California political column.*

*Crime reports from around the nation suggest that Satanism is increasingly linked to violent criminal activity such as child sexual abuse. Up to eight hundred crimes have been connected in some way to Satan worship. Authorities, however, are reluctant to assert publicly that a crime has been motivated by Satanist belief, in part for fear of provoking copycat crimes. For their part, many avowed Satanists deny that their religion promotes or condones such crimes.*

From small towns like Sanford, ME and big cities like San Francisco and Los Angeles, a steady stream of crime reports are indicating that satanism—devil worship—is becoming a fast-growing but still unmeasurable force in America.

When Richard Ramirez, the accused night stalker [1980s serial killer], raised his right hand in a Los Angeles courtroom, where he was accused of 14 murders and dozens of other felonies, his palm displayed an inked pentagram.

The five-pointed star within a circle positioned with two points up to symbolize the devil's horns was found at several night stalker murder scenes and the wife of one victim testified that Ramirez forced her to "swear on satan" she wouldn't alert neighbors by screaming.

In Huntington Beach, Calif., 33 small animals kept in an elementary school yard were slaughtered [in May 2003], a crime that police say was apparently part of a satanic ritual.

---

*As many as 800 crimes now under investigation ... are said to be linked somehow to devil worship.*

---

In Contra Costa County, Calif., the battered body of a 17-year-old boy who had graduated from playing "Dungeons and Dragons" to being involved with a satanic coven was found dead at the bottom of a cliff near San Francisco Bay [in 2002]. He had told his father and others that he wanted to leave the group.

Police call the death a suicide, but a coroner's report says the body bore marks more like those from a beating with sticks than bruises typically received in a fall.

Scores of reports link child molestations to satanic rituals featuring chalices of blood and participants either nude or wearing black hoods.

## Satanism and Crime

Altogether, as many as 800 crimes now under investigation by police nationwide are said to be linked somehow to devil worship.

Detectives from seven western states [in 2002] held a closed-door session to play strategies against satanism. One tactic they reportedly agreed upon: deny its involvement in crimes to discourage publicity and copycats.

Consistent with that idea, police and prosecutors are almost invariably hesitant to label devil-worship and sacrifice as the motive behind any crime and no one has been convicted of a crime on the basis of satanic involvement for more than a decade.

"There was talk about drinking blood and allegations that people involved worshipped the devil and had certain ceremonies," says Stephen Tauzer, a Bakersfield, Calif., prosecutor handling a case where as many as 80 adults have been suspected of molesting up to 60 children. "But we're not trying the case on religious grounds. I know satanism exists as a fad and that there are reports of cremated victims. But I have a hard time concluding that anything as large as cremating victims would not have witnesses."

Police usually say satanism exists, but has only peripheral involvement at most in crimes committed by alleged satanists. "One hears about cases," says Joseph Kranyak, a crime analyst for the San Bernardino, Calif., police department. "But when you track them down you find you're mostly chasing shadows. The vandalous nature of these things may not be organized and conspiratorial, but a response to stimuli like rock music."

And some of the leading fighters against satanism say there is a distinct difference between organized satanists like those belonging to San Francisco's Church of Satan and "freelance satanists." "In the formal churches, you get no murders, only symbolic actions," says Karen Hoyt, executive director of the Berkeley, Calif.–based Spiritual Counterfeits Project [an anti-occult ministry]. "But freelancers sacrifice animals and reportedly infants, although no one has found a body as yet."

## Satanic Bible

Church of Satan members adamantly deny any use of actual or animal sacrifice, although "The Satanic Bible" written by church founder Anton Lavey spells out rituals calling for "symbolic" human sacrifices.

"I'm a Satanist and I don't want to molest children," says Blanche Barton, Lavey's personal secretary. "The Satanic Bible says both animal and child sacrifices are illegal, so the whole idea of sacrificing to release energy is bull. But a lot of groups have adopted satanist images like hoods and gongs."

But the Satanic Bible does say that "Satan represents indulgence, instead of abstinence" and that "Satan represents all the so-called sins, as they all lead to physical, mental or emotional gratification." And in a chapter titled "On the Choice of a Human Sacrifice," Lavey adds that "Anyone who has wronged you" is a "fit and proper human sacrifice" and "you have every right to (symbolically) destroy them."

Opponents of satanism believe many "freelance" practitioners omit the admonition to make sacrifices "symbolic," and use the Satanic Bible to justify psychoses or perversions.

Covens centered around drugs, homosexuality, sexual fetishes, child molesting and other illicit activities are known to use rituals from the Satanic Bible and a later companion volume. So do groups using druidism, Celtic witchcraft and Egyptian mythology. Even "children's covens" are known to use such rituals.

Like many fundamentalists, Roger Burt, an Evangelical minister and president of the Christian Counseling Association in suburban Los Angeles, believes the current state of satanism is part of a long war between the forces of good and evil.

## Satanism's Attraction for Youths

"People who are getting involved in satanism are looking to get the power of demons and use it for themselves," he says. "It all centers on power over their peers, especially among teenagers, which is where this is growing fastest. This is not just a fad of the '80s. It is actual spiritual warfare. Spiritual possession has great power in attracting young people."

Games like Dungeons and Dragons, with medieval imagery, help attract children and teenagers to satanic rituals, which sometimes involve archaic dress. Rock music groups are even more of an influence, according to many police officials.

Burt lists heavy metal groups like AC/DC, Iron Maiden, Black Sabbath, Motley Crue, Blue Oyster Cult and Merciful Fate among the most influential. All have performed music with a satanic-style message that critics contend is taken literally by many listeners.

Burt says membership in satanic groups has grown to "at least 60,000," with about one-third in California, the world's main center of modern satanic activity. Hoyt and Burt agree that young children are often recruited by parents or teachers, then molested or forced to watch and participate in ritual killings of animals. Some are photographed during rituals and later blackmailed into continuing either via threats to show the pictures to parents or threats of harm to the parents.

Runaway teenagers, the anti-satanists say, are an especially fertile class of recruits. Other experts contend that many teenagers join satanist cults willingly.

"Many kids believe there is a force for evil in the world and some think it is the really powerful force in the universe," says Rabbi Jack Bemporad of Tenafly, N.J., a nationally known expert on cults. "A lot of them believe in demons, which are mentioned in the New Testament. Kids also have a lot of rage and anger and a feeling of powerlessness because of the threat of nuclear war and the increasing complexity of the world. They come to feel [that] if the world is going to destroy itself, they might as well glory in it."

In short, says Bemporad, they feel "if you can't beat evil, you might as well join it."

4

# Reports of Satanic Crimes
# Are Not Credible

*Cecil E. Greek*

*Cecil E. Greek is an associate professor of criminology at Florida State University.*

*The satanic panic in the 1980s generated disputable claims about Satanism, many of which were presented unquestioningly in the media. These claims included allegations of ritual child sacrifice. Yet crime statistics prove that such claims could not be true, and well-respected criminalists have concluded that these murders never took place.*

While satanic forces have been frequently blamed in Western history for the misfortunes of humankind, criminal justice officials in the U.S. have paid satanism little mind until the mid-1980s. At that point the country was swept by an epidemic of allegations that murders, sexual or ritual abuse of children, and ritual sacrifice of animals were commonplace activities among satanists. *Satan's Silence* is an investigation, co-authored by a journalist and an attorney, into a panic which swept the country regarding ritualistic abuse at daycare centers. However, as the authors suggest, fears of contemporary childhood victimization were part of a much larger satanic panic which swept the nation in the 1980s.... We will look at who spread of these beliefs, what was claimed, why they were believed, the problems with these accounts, and the

Cecil E. Greek, "Demonic Perspectives," College of Criminology and Criminal Justice, Florida State University, 2005. www.criminology.fsu.edu/crimtheory/week2.htm. Reproduced by permission.

continuing legacy of such beliefs. It is my opinion that the satanic panic represents the greatest crime hoax of this century, but one that continues to impact negatively on many people's lives.

## Media Role in Satanic Panic

The media helped to create a climate favorable to the belief that satanism had become a real-life menace. Gothic literature spawned horror comic books (banned in the 1950s), while Hollywood films featuring satanic themes have long been popular. Early on, sympathetic news reports spread belief in satanic crime, but as skepticism increased, the news media turned on those who claimed satanism was rampant in the country and asked for proof.

For this type of crime it was not newspapers or TV news, but TV talk shows which were the major media provider of information. TV talk shows like *Geraldo* [Rivera] and *Sally* [Jesse Raphael] featured this topic for a number of years and almost always uncritically presented the claims of widespread satanic abuse. Talk shows became the new medium for retelling "urban legends." Those like [coauthor of *Satan's Silence* Debbie] Nathan who have done a systematic investigation of the backgrounds of major writers and speakers on satanism, have found that many had questionable backgrounds or histories of mental illness. Such facts ought to have been discussed before anyone accepted at face value what these satanic storytellers were saying. However, Geraldo and other talk show hosts who had such speakers on their shows rarely if ever mentioned their backgrounds. Anti-satanists went unchallenged for the most part. This was not responsible journalism. On *Geraldo*, Geraldo ceased being a journalist, despite his claim that many of his shows represented "special investigative reports." The opposition point of view, when presented at all, was typically given to leaders of established Satanic churches like [founder of the Temple of Set, Michael] Aquino or [founder of the Church of Satan, Anton] LaVey rather than to nay-saying journalists or scholars. The "organized satanists," who claimed they had never murdered or tortured anyone, often were dismissed by audiences and opposition guests alike as obvious liars. Of course, everyone knows "satanists are liars." Talk shows do not present facts and validated information. They represent a new breed of TV, "info-tainment," presenting information as entertainment. They never should be assumed to have the same credibility as nightly newscasts or newspaper reports.

## Victims and Victimizers

Those claiming to have been victimized or victimizers (and sometimes both) in satanic groups included the following:

- *Children at daycare centers.* Children told hundreds of horrific tales; e.g., of being forced to commit sexual acts with robed, chanting adults; of being made to drink blood or eat feces; and to witness animal and human sacrifices. . . .

- *Teens who said they were satanists.* There is evidence that some teens spray-paint satanic graffiti on walls and even sadistically kill small animals in haphazardly concocted satanic rituals. But even reports of these incidents far outnumber their reality. A "self-styled satanist" is typically an isolated adolescent male who turns to the black arts. Some teenagers (particularly boys) are attracted to satanism. It offers an easy way to get the things teens want (power, money, sex). For this same reason boys form rock bands. Teens who feel alienated from their classmates may dabble in satanism, but most leave it rather quickly. However, a few do take the "theological" messages of satanism seriously. 17-year-old Sean Sellers claimed he was a satanist when he committed two murders in Oklahoma, but had a number of personal and family problems which might better explain his actions. Sellers acted on his own and was not doing the bidding of an organized satanic group.

• *Middle-aged women who in therapy (and often under hypnosis) stated they had recovered repressed memories of childhood satanic abuse.* They told stories of being "breeders" of babies born without official birth certificates so they could be ritually sacrificed to Satan; of how bodies were disposed of in such a way that no trace of their existence could ever be uncovered (corpses were burned and the bones ground into powder); and gruesome tales of cannibalism and blood drinking. Even though they had allegedly witnessed crimes, victims rarely reported them to the police after having recovered their memories. There has been considerable discussion of repressed memories since these reports surfaced and psychological experts on memory have found no evidence to support the phenomenon described by therapists. Also, those who study hypnosis warn of the dangers of trying to reintegrate victims diagnosed as suffering from multiple personality disorder or dissociative disorder. The newly integrated personality may end up believing that they experienced many things which never happened in all likelihood.

• *Ex-members of satanic covens who since had been converted to evangelical Christianity.* The most notable of these was Mike Warnke, who made an excellent living off telling already convinced Christian audiences that he was an ex-satanic high priest and participated in ritual victimizations. He was later exposed as a fraud. The only thing people who knew him as a teen agreed upon was that he had always had the ability to tell stories and make others believe them.

- *Members of organized satanic churches like the Church of Satan or Temple of Set.* These organizations are small in numbers and claim never to have murdered or tortured anyone. In terms of their life philosophy they are probably most similar to EST or any other self-awareness group which advocates putting one's own needs and desires first.

## People Who Claim They Have Exposed Satanic Crimes

1. *Cult cops.* Cops and ex-police officers charge fees to lecture audiences of other cops on what they "know" of satanic crime. *In Pursuit of Satan* by Robert Hicks debunks the cult cop phenomenon.

2. *Child interviewers, social workers and psychologists.* Treatment personnel lectured other child welfare workers on the dangers of satanic involvement. In November 1992, I attended a workshop sponsored by the Pinellas County [Florida] Juvenile Welfare Board on "Treatment Approaches: Adolescents and Cults." The workshop featured all the satanic hysteria one could ever want to endure.

3. *Psychiatrists interviewing middle-aged women.* A 1996 episode of [the PBS documentary series] *Frontline* documented how deeply psychiatry has been involved in the satanic panic. Women suffering from dissociative disorders who were referred to psychiatrists who believed in satanism were placed in very expensive treatment centers. They were informed they had been abused by satanic cults and had "secret codes" embedded in their memories which if activated would cause them to kill their husbands and children. Needless to say, husbands who believed this left their wives. Children were also alleged to be already initiated into a

satanic cult and placed in therapy as well. To date none of the doctors involved has been sued or had their licenses revoked.

---

*If satanism were as prevalent as anti-Satan experts claimed it was, bodies would have been unearthed everywhere.*

---

## The Claims Made About Satanism

Claims that were made stretched from tales of the use of the mass media (including computer games) to convert kids to satanism, to wholesale torture and murder, a massive cover-up, and a universal conspiracy. Rock music (particularly Heavy Metal), children's cartoons, and role-playing games were identified as gateways to satanism (similar to the way marijuana is singled out as a "gateway drug"). Music such as Ozzy Ozbourne's contained lyrics that overtly paid homage to the devil. An even more serious problem was "back masking." Alleged satanic messages were recorded backwards onto a record. The album didn't even have to be played backwards for the message to have its subliminal effect. It sunk into the subconscious and later resulted in negative behavior. The band Judas Priest was unsuccessfully sued by a parent who claimed the phrase "Do it" back masked onto an album had led her son to attempt suicide. No evidence for subliminal suggestion has been uncovered by psychologists. Children's cartoon's such as "He-Man" and "Thundercats" tapped into supernatural forces that detractors of the shows label satanic. Children who watched a steady diet of these cartoons were being set up to accept occult practices later as teens. The Internet may soon be recognized as the latest "doorway to hell."

If satanism were as prevalent as anti-Satan experts claimed it was, bodies would have been unearthed everywhere. Cult experts claimed there are anywhere from 50,000 to 2 million children ritually sacrificed to the devil each year. In comparison, only around 25,000 murders are reported in the U.S. each year. Almost all the alleged "missing" children can be accounted for as "kidnap" victims of one of the parents in a custody dispute. The FBI documents only about 100 stranger kidnappings of children each year.

Anti-satanists claimed that there was a vast organized network of devil worshippers in the U.S. that has infiltrated all levels of local, state, and federal government (including the criminal justice system.) Police officers refused to arrest and hid evidence; prosecutors would not indict; while judges who were part of the conspiracy refused to convict. Conspiracy theories of this nature are rarely if ever true. Other examples include the belief that gun control was a communist plot to have the American citizenry disarmed when the Russians would invade and house to house combat ensued; air pollution laws were generated by socialists who hope to speed up America's economic collapse, or that drugs are being used systematically by white elites to destroy black communities in America.

---

*While satanic crime may be largely mythical, the consequences of the satanic panic have been all too real.*

---

Why do people believe conspiracy theories? Hans Toch in *The Social Psychology of Social Movements* analyzed the psychological gratifications that conspiracy theories offer, whether of the left-wing or right-wing variety. They allow individuals who believe in them to have one all-encompassing answer to a myriad of social problems. A conspiracy theory also allows those who believe it to "know" the future before it happens. Such knowledge allows them to feel secure while others struggle to understand what is going on around them. Critics have argued that the satanism phenomenon was largely the result of ultra-right-wing fundamentalist and evangelical

Christians spreading their ideas concerning the "end times." If Satan's power is growing, the Judgment Day is near. But, as we have seen it was also supported by the welfare establishment and some branches of psychiatry.

While at first law enforcement agencies took the reports of murdered infants seriously, they gradually realized there was no evidence of these events. Kenneth Lanning of the FBI wrote a series of articles concluding that no such murders had occurred. However, true believers still exist. A TV program on Satan broadcast on a religious channel in January 1996 repeated many of the same accusations that law enforcement investigators and scholars have been unable to validate for 10 years. These claims put investigators in the unenviable position of trying to disprove a negative. How would one prove Earth has never been visited by UFOs?

While satanic crime may be largely mythical, the consequences of the satanic panic have been all too real. As Nathan and [coauthor Michael R.] Snedeker documented [in *Satan's Silence*] hundreds of adults were falsely convicted, many children suffered months of excruciating interviews in which they were "forced" to confess to things which never occurred and then put into unnecessary treatment programs, and the lives of thousands of families were needlessly disrupted.

# 5

# Satanism Promotes a Culture of Death

*Jim Howell*

*Jim Howell works as a journalist for United Press International.*

*Adherents of the Church of Satan claim that their religion has a liberating effect on its members. A number of grisly crimes linked to Satanism, however, show that it actually promotes a culture of death that can enslave lonely young people who may need spiritual guidance from mainstream religious clergy.*

Satanism is growing so quickly worldwide that ... a papal university in Rome will offer courses on this frightening phenomenon. According to Vatican sources, divinity students at the pontifical Regina Apostolorum (Queen of the Apostles) University will learn about devil worship, witchcraft, demonology and exorcism.

They will learn to give pastoral care to youngsters who have joined satanic cults, but also to their worried parents, a Vatican prelate told United Press International.

## Satanism Gets More Internet Hits

Type the word "Satanism" into the Google search engine, and some 461,000 hits will appear on your computer's monitor. That's more than the terms, "Lutheranism" and "Calvinism," the two oldest Protestant traditions, will produce—together.

The U.S.-based "Church of Satan," which has about 10,000 members, shows up 56,000 times on Google, compared with the Evangelical Lutheran Church in America's [ELCA] measly 15,000 hits, even though the ELCA counts nearly 5 million faithful. "Of course such figures reveal little about a subject's real importance," says the Rev. Albrecht Immanuel Herzog, executive vice president of a based mission society headquartered in Neuendettelsau, Bavaria.

---

*It is the Internet that . . . attracts the world's young to the Prince of Darkness.*

---

On the other hand, the figures certainly do show one thing: In a global society dominated by the Internet, the devil and the occult garner a considerably greater interest right now than Lutheran or Calvinist theologies—or Methodism, for that matter (245,000 hits).

It is the Internet that, along with "black metal"–type rock music and its chilling lyrics, attracts the world's young to the Prince of Darkness [Satan].

## Youth's Attraction to Satanism

What makes them such easy prey? Loneliness, according to Italian professor Carlo Climati, who will teach the course at Regina Apostolorum—loneliness of the juvenile Internet surfer.

Thus while the "Church of Satan," which advertises itself as a mix of hedonistic philosophy with the rituals of black magic, claims to liberate its adherents (from traditional stuffiness), Satanism really does not cater to a thirst for freedom, says the Rev. Herzog.

"Instead, it aims at a desire for dependency and thus enslaves," he goes on. It is hard to argue with Herzog on this point since many Satanism Web sites are directly linked to others featuring bondage, discipline, sadomasochism and violent death, including photographs of aborted embryos in garbage cans.

---

*Gruesome incidents linked to Satanism worldwide proves that this is the true locus of the "culture of death."*

---

## Satanism's Culture of Death

A cursory glance of gruesome incidents linked to Satanism worldwide proves that this is the true locus of the "culture of death" Pope John Paul II never cease[d] to denounce. In recent years, these things occurred, for example:

- In Trier, Germany, birthplace of Karl Marx, the prosecutor's office has been investigating the claim of a woman that babies were being cut up and eaten in Satanist rituals.

- In Finland a youthful pair was jailed for eating part of a fellow devil worshiper's body, abusing it sexually, then cutting it into small pieces, all to the tunes of Black Metal music—and all in a Satanist ritual.

- In Brisbane, Australia, two young sadistic lesbians were sentenced for stabbing and slashing the throat of a 59-year-old New Zealand grandmother—in a Satanist ritual.

- In Athens, young Satanists were sentenced for stripping, cuffing, raping and slaughtering a 15-year-old girl—in a Satanist initiation scene.

- In Buenos Aires, Argentina, two young women were found guilty of killing their father and stabbing him in the face 100 times—in a Satanist family event of sorts.

- In Donskoi, Russia, Satanists led by 80-year-old Yelena Kuzina and including members as young as 20 were jailed for murders committed in occult rituals.

- Only recently in a forest near Milan, Italy, youngsters danced on the graves of two coreligionists they had just killed—in a Satanist ritual murder.

These examples can be continued ad infinitum. "This phenomenon," a Catholic exorcist told United Press International some time ago, "is a growth industry for the pastoral care business, if only there were enough ministers prepared to deal with this situation—and to read the alarm signal when young people suddenly act strangely, walk around in black gear with chains and spikes, and hide their faces under grisly black makeup.

"Don't think this is in all cases just a form of entertainment," he warned. "It can be a sign of an enslavement to a growing lethal faith."

# 6

# Satanists Say Their Religion Is Misunderstood

*Ed Power*

*Ed Power is a writer and contributor to the* Irish Independent *newspaper.*

*Church of Satan members assert that portrayals of their religion as one of violent ritualism are false. Instead, they say, Satanism promotes self-gratification and is centered around the natural instincts and desires of man. Many Satanists do not even believe in the existence of Satan, although they may use him as a symbol of free will and thought.*

Hell hath no fury like the satanist scorned—judging by the mood of Devil worshippers this week. Their anger came after a British sailor was given official sanction to practise satanism on board a ship in the Royal Navy. Although satanists are grateful for the decision, the media backlash and public outcry over the decision, and the ensuing negative portrayal of their religion as little more than ritual blood drinking, infant sacrifice and black masses, has the group up in arms.

## What Satanists Really Believe

Members of the Church of Satan (estimated worldwide membership—25,000) insist that these claims of murderous ritualism are dark propaganda and a cruel slur on their faith. Satanism, they say, is the religion of self gratification, of ca-

Ed Power, "Don't Call Us Evil ... We're Just Satanists," *Irish Independent*, October 29, 2004. Reproduced by permission.

pitulation to the primal instinct. Snatch away the arcane trap-
pings and there is very little of the occult to it. In fact, many
satanists insist they do not even believe in the Devil as normally understood.

Rather than bending the knee to a horned Antichrist, the
figure they worship is—with apologies to [rock band] INXS—
'the devil inside'. Satan, they explain, resides in each of us—he
is our inclination to anger, to seek revenge, to follow our most
base impulse regardless of the emotional harm to others. The
satanist merely accepts, indeed revels in, the sordidness of human inclination. That he or she sets about this with a theatri-
cal flair—black robes, chalk-drawn pentagrams and female
nakedness are the staple of its rituals—is largely a question of
personal taste.

"The popular notion that satanism is defined as the worship of Satan or the Devil is disputed by many satanists," ex-
plains 'Dorchas', an Irish satanist, on her website. "The more
generally accepted definition among them is that satanism is a
religion that is based on man's natural instincts and desires.
They do not worship the Christian Devil; many satanists do
not believe in Satan at all."

---

*Followers of the Devil are . . . free thinkers rebelling
against the modern world and its veneer of decency.*

---

Other satanists are aghast at being portrayed as unhinged
exhibitionists and molesters of women and children. "We do
not murder children, kill animals or do weird things to vir-
gins," fumes one website.

Devil worship as practised by Dorchas and her Coven Of
Bel Fire appears to owe more to pagan than Judeo-Christian
tradition (although 'mainstream' pagans blanch at the comparison and disavow any connection). The Satan to whom
Dorchas pays homage is not the seductive sprite that sought
to lead astray Jesus in the desert or lured the citizens of Salem

into witchcraft. He is, if not a benign figure, then at least an indifferent one, an embodiment of animal urges rather than a scheming nemesis of Christ.

Followers of the Devil are, she says, free thinkers rebelling against the modern world and its veneer of decency. "To many satanists, Satan is used as a symbol for mankind's natural desires, instincts and free thought," she writes. "They believe that all people should have the freedom to do as their will leads them so long as it does not affect an unwilling person or animal. They are free thinkers and regard ourselves as their own gods. They see regular rules and ideas as pointless and challenge anything that they do not agree with. They believe in following their own rules."

## The Dark Side of Satanic Beliefs

Yet while satanists insist they pose no threat to the community, some believe their beliefs cast a pernicious shadow. "You do get teenagers dabbling in Ouija boards and animal sacrifice. Sometimes it is curiosity got out of hand, but there can be long-term emotional damage," says Mike Garde of Dialogue Ireland, a group that promotes "awareness and understanding of new religious organisations" (Satanism is not expressly outlawed in Ireland though rituals that break the law obviously are).

"In part it is natural curiosity on the part of some young teenagers who have been raised as Catholics. Many mess with Ouija boards and there seems to be no long-term harmful effect. They may as well have been playing Monopoly. However, there are cases where this sort of thing can lead to far more extreme behaviour and may tip people over the edge."

The desecration of graves in Dublin several years ago was, he believes, the work of organised satanists. When the Irish are drawn to satanism it is not because of an excess of religion in their upbringing—which may have been a factor in the past—but, says Garde, for precisely the opposite reason.

Our lives are increasingly bereft of spiritual context, creating space for the amoral self-gratification of the satanic creed.

"The decline of religion has left a vacuum and there are a lot of people out there who feel spiritually disenfranchised. Satanism is the answer for a few."

## Anton LaVey and Contemporary Satanism

Satanism is generally held to be almost as old as Christianity, although many once tarred as devil worshippers are now thought to have been pagans opportunistically slandered by the arriving monotheists. Yet the roots of contemporary devil worship stretch back only to 1966, when Anton LaVey, a charismatic hedonist, established the Church of Satan in San Francisco.

A classic product of time and context, LaVey's cult drew on the anti-establishment fervour of the 1960s, owing little to classical occultists, such as Aleister Crowley and the Marquis de Sade. Like them, though, freedom—sexual freedom in particular—is the core of LaVey's theology.

LaVey stressed that his is primarily a religion of individualism. Causing physical harm is expressly forbidden in his most famous text, *The Satanic Bible*. Nor is kindness towards others in conflict with devilry; as generosity to loved ones increases personal happiness it chimes with LaVey's core credo—indulge in whatever makes you feel good.

In an ironic echoing of the American religious right, LaVey had an abiding hatred of Hollywood, which he blamed for stoking anti-satanic rhetoric in movies such as *The Exorcist* (though that didn't prevent him from claiming to have worked on Roman Polanski's 1960s chiller *Rosemary's Baby*).

However, LaVey's apostles are not always as sanguine. In 2002, a German satanist, Manuela Ruda, and her husband, Daniel, admitted the ritual killing of a friend, Frank Haagen, who was stabbed 66 times. Ruda had told the court that she became a satanist during a visit to Britain. Recent ritualised attacks on horses in the UK have also been blamed on satanic practices.

The notion of a devil waiting in the dark to tempt you astray is long rejected by most people, even those of faith. Yet if you interpret satanism strictly as a philosophy rather than a vein of Christian mythology, you might conclude that the dark one has already triumphed, suggests Mike Garde.

What, he asks, is the materialism currently sweeping Irish society but the purest manifestation of the satanists' mantra—that individual gratification is a goal to be pursued regardless of how others are affected?

7

# Satanism Promotes Ritual Violence

## Harun Yahya

*Harun Yahya is a pen name of a Turkish author who has written numerous books on politics, religious faith, and science.*

*Satanism is a twisted belief system that ritualizes violence and cruelty. Satanists worship and justify both violence and immorality. They also reject religious-based values and all rules and boundaries. Such beliefs lead logically to acts of sexual perversion, human torture, and even murder as forms of worship.*

Satanism is a perverted ideology that makes violence and savagery a ritual in its creed. Satanists, who describe themselves as such, make deeds of inhumanity and brutality into acts of worship.

When the word *Satanism* is mentioned most people think merely of its widespread psychological influence on young people, and regard it as a kind of insignificant mystical movement. Also, due to the influence of the media, they may think of Satanists as performing strange rituals, much unlike what ordinary and well-balanced people would otherwise do. It is true that Satanists are part of a culture of violence and perform strange and horrible rites, yet, what most people fail to see is that Satanism is a materialist and atheist ideology that supports violence and which dates back to the 1800s. Furthermore, the ideology has a large number of followers throughout the world.

Harun Yahya, from *Terrorism: The Ritual of the Devil.* New Delhi, India: Islamic Book Service, 2002, pp. 90–93, 97–101. Reproduced by permission.

The fundamental principle of Satanism is that it rejects all religious values, takes the Devil as its deity, and claims that hell is a kind of salvation. According to the belief of Satanism, people have no responsibilities, apart from that of following their own desires. If his desires lead a person to anger, hatred, revenge, deceit, theft, the harming of others or even murder, then that is acceptable. The basic logic that Satanism relies on, in support of that belief, is the claim that the avoidance of evil is a kind of insincerity. In other words, this perverted belief maintains that if his desires impel someone to kill another, and if he acts according to that impulse, then he has behaved sincerely.

Virtues such as love, tolerance, patience and forgiveness, which are highly esteemed by most people, and are elements of the true morality, are loathed by Satanists. This deviant ideology maintains that there should be no restrictions on evil and such feelings as hatred, anger and vengeance. Article 5 of *The Satanic Bible* widely regarded as the fundamental textbook of Satanism, states, instead of the biblical principle that says "To him who strikes you on the cheek, offer the other also," that "Satan represents vengeance, instead of turning the other cheek." Elsewhere in that same book appears the commandment:

> "Hate your enemies with a whole heart, and if a man smite you on one cheek, SMASH him on the other!"

It is obvious that according to such thinking it will be impossible to prevent any kind of wickedness. Such an atmosphere will inevitably lead to chaos and strife. It is impossible to speak of order, peace, stability, security, forgiveness or tolerance in any society in which people do not listen to the voice of their consciences, and are thus unable to distinguish between good and bad, and to use their will and judgment to act for good. In an environment of that sort, anyone who feels anger towards somebody else will be unable to restrain that anger and behave with moderation, and will inevitably seek his revenge. Alternatively, instead of being patient in times of need and poverty, and attempting to address those needs in a sensible manner, these people will resort to theft and other sorts of crime. Satanism is their justification for doing so.

## Satanism's Refusal to Recognize Rules or Bounds

The kind of society proposed by the ideology of Satanism recognizes no rules and no bounds. Its aim is the free expression of selfish desires and evil. In his book *The Satanic Bible*, Anton LaVey, regarded as the founder of modern Satanism, recommends to his followers that they live by and promote wickedness as they so please. In an interview, LaVey even said: "I feel laws are, obviously, made to be broken. . . . I see nothing wrong with robbing somebody on the street."

Satanism's refusal to recognize any bounds does not stop there, of course. People would not only harm themselves and those around them, but would direct their hostility and anger at all. That refusal to recognize any limits, moreover, leads to the regard of violence as an intrinsic part of life. According to Satanism, violence is a fact of nature, and thus inescapable. Therefore, this distorted view maintains that it is perfectly permissible for people to resort to violence. Since any attempt to prevent or minimize violence is a violation of what is natural, any attempt to do so is futile, and it is therefore illogical to do so.

As we have seen, Satanism holds utterly perverse beliefs, which encourage people to be aggressive, to commit murder, and even mass slaughter. In America in particular, academics have established that Satanism lies at the root of national terror, and that serious steps need to be taken in order to deal with it. One of these academics is Carl Roschke, a professor at Denver University, who has stressed the importance of the subject in the words, "We're really dealing with the way satanic ideology has become a basis for domestic terrorism." Roschke says that the most important step in the war to be waged against Satanism is to make it clear that its followers are not just "harmless wackoes," but that when their crimes are examined, one can understand just how harmful someone claiming to be a Satanist can be. . . .

*One can recognize such perversion, immorality and savagery in any society that takes Satan as its guide.*

## Satanist Rituals

Black masses, and the terrible things that are conducted during them, is what most often comes to peoples' minds whenever Satanism is mentioned. Yet, many people believe that it is make-believe only portrayed in films, and that nothing of the sort actually takes place in real life. However, the terrible scenes we are used to watching in films are really parts and aspects of Satanist masses and rituals.

The real purpose behind these rituals is to make contact with the Devil and learn his so-called teachings. In order to see just how important these devilish rites are in Satanism, a brief look at their own books and websites is more than sufficient. The common feature of these publications is the way they devote considerable space to gloomy subjects and insist on the importance of the black mass. In a well-known Satanist website, which carries various Satanist messages for the under-18s, these so-called masses are emphasized as being one of the fundamental elements of Satanism, and that young people who cannot attend group ceremonies should nevertheless hold such services on their own. The details of the services these young people are instructed to hold are then given:

> Don't be disturbed or frightened or think you're crazy when you feel contacted by the Dark Ones. . . . Approach the Dark Masters with the proper degree of respect and decorum—

that's what rituals are for, to establish a relationship. . . . You don't need everything mentioned in Dr. LaVey's books to do an effective ritual. Maybe you don't have the money to obtain, or the private space to store, items such as swords, chalices, black robes, gongs and elaborate altars. Here is a powerful ritual you can perform. . . . Light the candle and set it before you. . . . As you gaze at the flame, say in your mind or out loud, "I am ready, oh, Dark Lord. I feel your strength within me and wish to honor you in my life. I am one of the Devil's Own. Hail Satan!" . . . This is a simple way of conjuring Satan into your life.

One can recognize such perversion, immorality and savagery in any society that takes Satan as its guide. For Satanists, these things are inspired by the Devil himself, and must be adhered to. Satanists who do adhere to them fall into forms of sexual perversions, torture humans as well as animals, and even perform such disgusting things as the drinking of the blood of the creatures or people they kill. In many countries of the world, young people who describe themselves as Satanists hold drug-parties at which all kinds of immorality and perversion take place, and which frequently end in the killing of one of their number in the Devil's name.

The way Satanists attach such importance to the shedding of blood at their rituals is a small-scale example of the plan Satan has for mankind. Satan hates mankind, and wants to inflict as much suffering on it as possible. It is therefore his aim to fill the world with bloodshed. The ideologies of the Antichrist . . . such as fascism, racism and communism, all serve his purpose. All the wars, massacres, killings, and acts of terrorism, linked to these and similar atheistic ideologies, are all "Satanic masses" aimed at satisfying the Devil's lust for blood.

Those who openly describe themselves as Satanists carry out the shedding of blood as an act of worship. Those who incite terror and anarchy in the world are actually performing the same rite, in more secret but with far wider ramifications.

In short, the Devil, and the system of the Antichrist established by him for the world are using those they have managed to take in and are trying to turn the world into a brutal battleground.

8

# Satanists Use Violence Only for Self-Defense

*Vexen Crabtree*

*Vexen Crabtree is a registered member of the Church of Satan.*

*Because violence is a fact of life, Satanism's teaching of violent retribution against assailants is more beneficial than Christianity's emphasis on turning the other cheek. In the Satanist view, violence as retribution is a form of social justice. Satanism does not promote random violence. But force is necessary for self-preservation in some situations and ensures that individuals will suffer the consequences of their actions.*

What does Satanism teach about violence? First I state that violence occurs in real life and therefore *an approach to violence* is necessary. Then I describe the comments on violence in The Satanic Bible and compare them to Christianity and Judaism. The apparent hardness of Satanism is then examined in more detail. I give some examples of violence and conclude that Satanism has a more valid and productive approach to violence than Christianity, Judaism or Pacifism.

## Violence Happens

Satanism is a religion of real life. Violence, in real life, happens. People have always fought each other, and in my opinion people always will do [so]. Satanists know that violence

Vexen Crabtree, "Satanism and Violence," *Satanism*, 2002. www.dpjs.co.uk/violence.html.

50

happens. It doesn't matter how moral, advanced or clever you are, sometimes you will be destroyed by someone simply because they are stronger than you. A Satanist feels that he is certainly worth preserving. It is only common sense that even a small amount of combat skill can safeguard yourself against unfortunate turns of events. . . .

## Satanism, Christianity, and Judaism on Violent Retribution

I will briefly contrast the apparent harshness of the Satanic teachings on violent retribution to those of Christianity and Judaism, and proceed in the next section to justify how I believe Satanism is superior to those by comparing them all to social pacifism.

*Satanism.* Of the Nine Satanic Statements:

5. Satan represents vengeance, instead of turning the other cheek!

and of the Eleven Satanic Rules of the Earth:

11. When walking in open territory, bother no one. If someone bothers you, ask him to stop. If he does not stop, destroy him.

and from the Book of Satan:

"If a man smite you on one cheek, SMASH him on the other! Smite him hip and thigh! [. . .] Give blow for blow, scorn for scorn, doom for doom—with compound interest liberally added thereunto! [. . .] Make yourself a Terror to your adversary, and when he goeth his way, he will possess much additional wisdom to ruminate over. Thus shall you make yourself respected in all the walks of life, and your spirit [. . .] shall live, not in an intangible paradise, but in the brains and sinews of those whose respect you have gained."

"Blessed are the bold, for they shall be masters of the world—Cursed are the righteously humble, for they shall be trodden under cloven hoofs!"

*Christianity.* The comment on "turning the other cheek" in the fifth Satanic Statement is commentary on Christianity: "You have heard it said, 'An eye for an eye, and a tooth for a tooth'. But I say do not resist evil. Who smites you on one cheek, offer to him the other. And he who takes away your cloak, tell him also to take away your coat."

This has Christians offer themselves as victims instead of executing social justice. This is surely a prescription for social disaster! This selfish abstinence, the point of which is to go to Heaven, is a detriment to society, and most Christians I know would not actually uphold this statement to be true and certainly don't act by it. Those criminals that would destroy society would be given free reign, which is *wrong*. Punishment, 'resistance', is most definitely more moral than abstinence.

*Judaism.* The author of text that Matthew and Mark quoted from when he mentioned 'an eye for an eye' was making a reference to the *Jewish Law* of the Old Testament. Is it true, therefore, that these statements in the Satanic Bible are close to Judaism? I believe not. The '*eye for an eye*' statement in the Torah is actually part of a guideline stating the punishment should fit the crime. The Torah and Rabbis would also apply *grace* to this, meaning that the actual punishment was normally not as severe as it could be. I personally *do* believe in applying grace to retribution *however*: I think it is also right to exact an unmerciful revenge when the situation warrants it. However, this is rarely needed and frequently illegal—so gauge the consequences of your actions carefully, people!

## Satanism and Violence

*How can there be peace in a Satanic world?* What a question! How can there be peace in a theistic world? Where anybody can kill in the name of some god and claim divine right? The monotheistic Churches have caused wars, divisions and torture. Yes, firstly [before] I start I would very much like to point out that all religious teachings have caused violence, sometimes on a quite large scale. I fully expect that sometimes Satanic teachings will, too, cause unwanted violence.

Secondly—do you really think that Human Beings are capable of not fighting one another? As we pointed out in the first section, violence *happens* and frequently it is through no choice of our own. We need to be taught how to respond, what to do . . . 'turn the other cheek' is probably the least useful thing, personally or socially, that can be done when faced with violence. It is clear that pacifism is not an option.

---

*The main way to curb behavior is to make it clear that people* will *pay the consequences of their actions.*

---

## Satanism Advocates Retribution Against Assailants

Criminals, which for simplicity I am defining here as those whose actions will undermine society, cannot be allowed to go unchecked. In this much, nearly everyone is agreed. Something must be done. However, that 'thing' is almost certainly never entirely efficient, and it *is* up to the general populace to look after themselves. Society does not magically hold itself together: It is held together by *human strength* and *values*. These values must be defended. Criminals must *know* that society is against them. The more feeble the populace are, the more powerful criminals become and the less stable the society is. Society degenerates when people no longer pay the consequences of their own actions.

The main way to curb behavior is to make it clear that people *will* pay the consequences of their actions. *Turning the other cheek* is simply not a moral option. We should be resolved to help people and bring them up to standard, but the best way *any* animal learns is that *as soon* as it does something wrong it is punished. The longer the delay between the action and the punishment, the less effective that punishment is. Indeed, I believe it is even immoral to punish a person for a crime too long after they have committed it. Pacifism and *meekness* do not hold together society.

Without punishment for the wrongs people do, even on a personal level, we allow ourselves to be run over. We allow the wrongs of society to multiply. Two wrongs don't necessarily make a right—but if a person would commit three wrongs, and you punish them (and therefore stop them) after the first the overall total of wrongs is actually one less than it would have been otherwise.

Although the term *self respect* has been hijacked as a macho street term, it is what these teachings boil down to. You do not let yourself get trampled on, and when you see a wrong you take the responsibility to immediately destroy the threat. This gives rise to the male 'street talk' of Satanism, the instinctive and automatic retribution to those who do wrong: especially strangers and random assailants.

I do not interpret "destroy" to mean "kill", as this would be stupid to kill those who merely bother me. I interpret this to mean that you should not take any shit whilst going about your life. Don't let yourself get trampled on. "Destroy" means that you remove that person as a risk. To satisfy this rule you will need to make yourself strong: Emotionally and physically capable of dealing with antagonizers. Such self preservation is essential to dealing with the unknowns of life.

*Self Defence.* It is a teaching of Satanism, a teaching of [Satanist] Vexen [Crabtree] that all people should invest in self defence. All people should *learn about violence*, experience it, witness it, so that they can best deal with it when it surfaces randomly.

Is a Kung Fu master more or less violent than an uneducated thug? He is less violent, of course, because like mature Satanists, he understands violence and when it is or isn't necessary. Violence, as an increased-odds methodology, is often avoided for much more intelligent methods of retribution, or preservation.

*Satanism in Practice.* Satanism is much less conducive to random violence, as a Satanist always keeps in mind that he alone bears the results of his actions, both in the long and short term. "Responsibility to the responsible!" is the 6th Satanic Statement. Balance is a key factor, something severely missing from monotheistic Churches past and present.

We'd rather leave the world as it is instead of reducing it to dust. Stability benefits all but there cannot be total peace: we are honest. Most Satanists live peaceful, stable, happy lives. The myth of Satanic violence evaporates—it simply doesn't happen. It is this fact that proves that the Satanist's attitude to violence is correct.

## How Satanists Should Handle Violent Situations

*[Example]: The Columbine girl.* [Witness reported] . . . when [the gunman] asked [Cassie Bernall, who was killed in the 1999 shooting at Columbine High School in Littleton, Colorado] whether she believed in God, "Bernall said she believed in Jesus Christ as her Lord and Saviour, and was shot in the temple."

When armed gunmen are killing everyone, there is only one *true, brave* and *correct* course of action. If it is immoral for them to be doing what they are doing, because they are killing innocent people, then it is not moral to help them in their activity. It is most correct to *take them on*, to attack them. If possible, run away. It is better for everyone to escape rather than unnecessarily risk lives. If you cannot run away, if you are cornered or singled out, you *must* destroy your assailants.

In many circumstances, trying to talk to them is successful. Columbine was *not* one of those circumstances.

The most moral course of action, the one that shows you care more for human life than your own is to take on the assailants. Even if it is unlikely, there is still a *chance*. Hopefully you will achieve something, even if it is just wasting their time, ammo and reserve strength, you will have helped others. But why did Cassie Bernall not do this? This is the question I am asking—what went wrong?

First of all, none of the staff nor students attacked the gunmen either. I believe that all the victims during the attack were too scared and too confused. Children especially are not mentally equipped to deal with this type of event. The adult staff have less of an excuse. All in all, the chances are that none of them had training, or, certainly, none of them had the experience required to keep a cool head during violent events. It is this *losing of cool* that kills most people in all violent situations. From panic, freezing and irrational actions, *keeping a cool head* seems to be the most important override. This is achieved, hopefully, by some physical training and at the very least some instruction on how to control your thoughts during times of intense and unexpected pressure. This is not something that we expect to be taught in schools.

Satanism is a religion that teaches people about real life. Satanists know that religion is probably the most fucked up invention of mankind. That more violence occurs in the name of religion than any other single reason. A Satanist knows that when a gunman asks you, "Are you a Satanist?" the response is *not*: "I am a Satanist! Hail Satan!" The Satanist knows the response is: "No!—what?"

In the name of peace, for love of man, the Satanist knows and is taught that *lying* is not a black or white issue. Cassie was under no moral obligation to tell her attacker the truth. She certainly had *some bravery*. Suicide, I believe, requires *some bravery*. But the *ultimate* act of goodness is to fight life's problems head on—suicide is a second best to soldiering on. Her loved ones, her family and those who care about her (and even strangers who are moved by her fate) all mourn her. Upset and suffering have been created.

For some reason, she was more interested in proclaiming her religious beliefs than she was in protecting herself or others. I believe in times of stress it is frequently our instincts that take over. Most people get frozen with fear. Cassie was not frozen with fear—she was filled with enough pride in her religious belief to stand up and say *precisely* what it took (and more) to get her shot. If her beliefs were in *life*, that was *not* the right course of action.

Self preservation had taken a back seat in her mind. This is not the sign of a person resorting to instinct, but of someone with their instincts overridden. Martial training can provide that level of cool, but martial training is geared towards self preservation. Satanism provides Satanists with an instinctive ability to lie about their religion. Cassie's religious beliefs, though, were what had overridden her instincts. Those beliefs, when put into practice, turned out to be self destructive.

Rather than try and reduce the suffering in the school (by trying to save herself or others) her ego decided it would be better to promote her theology rather than save lives. From Mother Theresa to Jesus Christ, religious adherents have been failing to protect humanity for the same reasons. Theology becomes more important than life or logic.

Satanism teaches:

1. Lying can save lives
2. Dogma costs lives
3. Dramatic religious statements at the wrong time are self destructive

4. Beliefs that are not borne of self preservation are self destructive and immoral as they will cause suffering and pain amongst those who love and care for you. . . .

## Revenge and Self-Preservation

A neophyte emailed me about an incident from "years ago" when he was attacked by a gang of drug dealers. I do not know whether he had prior involvement with them, or what, but he appeared to know them.

> "I have read the Satanic Bible and have a good understanding. In the Nine Satanic Statements, #5 it says "Satan represents vengeance, instead of turning the other cheek." but also says that the Satanist practices self preservation. I took no further action against these people. Going a step farther would have surely gotten me in over my head, either with the gang, or the authorities, and interfere with my schooling. Going after them, in my opinion would be stupid.
>
> "Your input would be greatly appreciated."

My response was:

> "You can redirect vengeance however you want. You could redirect it into a general fight against drugs and violent gangs, or you could actively investigate the drug dealer and gang yourself, and see if you can damage them, in true vigilante fashion. Do whatever it is within your capabilities to do, but, as you point out, don't do anything stupid. Looking after yourself is more important than going to crusades to sort out other people. As a Satanist, your own existence is important; preserve yourself first. If you destroy yourself on some mad mission to attack a gang of practiced and violent drug dealers, then you've done no good. Be a tactician *and* a hero, not a fool.
>
> "In short—your instincts seem to be right.
>
> "Hail Satan!"

As it exclaims in The Satanic Bible, Book of Lucifer, 2nd chapter: "I am a Satanist! Bow down, for I am the highest embodiment of Human life!" Don't waste that life on pointless, short-term goals that reduce your ability to live a strong life. Fight when you have to—but don't invite your own doom!

If we do dispense of violence . . . then it would only manifest itself in different ways or sports. Violence *within* people's own reality would still be yearned for, generated conflict would still exist—at least, for many people. Perhaps, though, at this or some point of human development, technology or science can remove our instincts towards violence and our ability to behave violently. Until then, however, the Satanic attitude to violence is perhaps one of the most obvious, common sense and strangely *least dangerous* and least self deluded attitude.

No matter how you look at it, sometimes force is required. The Satanist may never engage in violence, but there is always the chance that one day he will have to! It is the same for all people, and as a religion of the Earth, Satanism in the name of intelligence requires we are able to physically defend ourselves.

# 9

# The Negative Aspects of Satanism Outweigh the Positives

*D. Rebecca Deinsen*

*D. Rebecca Deinsen is a priest with the Episcopal Church of the United States. She has a bachelor of arts degree in religion and philosophy as well as two master's degrees in religious studies.*

*Satanism possesses several positive features, including honesty, independence, and nonconformity. However, Satanism also warrants criticism for being reactionary, not very intellectual, overly dependent on emotions, and restricted by a surplus of rhetoric. Worst of all, the belief that Satanists are superior to practitioners of other religions requires a high degree of self-deception.*

Without exception, the people I've met who consider themselves Satanists in the tradition of Anton LaVey are some of the most interesting people I've met. They tend to be ethical, intelligent, confident, honest, and nice . . . ooops . . . I mean evil! And a read through the Satanic Bible [SB] is enough to convince critics and skeptics alike that Anton LaVey was brilliant (besides being funny and brazen) in his own right. Yet, I still find much to be desired in modern Satanism and offer the following essay to Satanists and would-be Satanists alike as an honest critique.

*For those unfamiliar with LaVeyan Satanism, please note that Satanists are atheists and do not believe in a real Satan/ Devil.*

D. Rebecca Deinsen, "Why I'm Not a Satanist," *Franciscan-Anglican.com*, 2004. www.franciscan-anglican.com/Not_A_Satanist.htm. Reproduced by permission of the author.

## Satanism's Positive Aspects

*1. The Honesty.* Satanism strives to be purely honest. It tells it like it is! A true Satanist does not stand for hypocrisy in others or in oneself. Satanism is a breath of fresh air in a society so tainted with blatant hypocrisy, the discrepancy between teaching and action.

*2. The Independent Thought.* Satanism requires one to think for oneself and this has a way of separating the intelligent from the stupid. Satanists understand the value of independent thought and are allowed to analyze and choose what to believe and do according to their own values and interests, not merely those instilled in them by social norms and culture.

---

*Satanism lights a fire of passion and offers a sense of purpose.*

---

*3. The In-Your-Face Nonconformity.* Satanists have practically invented new rules when it comes to nonconformity. I enjoy the fact that the average unthinking person is either offended or afraid of Satanists and their symbols. [Satanism], like many alternative cultures and philosophies, unabashedly stands over and against the conforming masses of society while simultaneously challenging them, it just does so more extravagantly.

*4. Self-Empowerment.* In a world where people are often driven to feel ashamed, guilty, or just plain negative about themselves, Satanism offers a key to uplift the individual to new heights of self-confidence, value, and consequently, empowerment. Satanists value themselves and embrace their own power and talents; they not only acknowledge them, they flaunt them. Most people long for the ability to embrace themselves in such overwhelmingly positive terms but cannot and will not. The Satanist can and does—and doesn't hide it!

*5. Ethical but Not Dogmatic.* Satanism offers a minimum ethical structure and trusts individuals enough to figure the rest out for themselves. This means that the average Satanist must, once again, think for themselves. This generally results in a more well-reasoned, sensible, and sophisticated ethical way of life than the average person. Most Satanists are ethical and moral, but not out of guilt or conformity, they are so out of common sense.

---

*Satanism is overwhelmingly reactionary.*

---

*6. It's Just So Much More Interesting.* Yeah, this is one of my shallow reasons. But one has to admit, it's much more intriguing and it raises all kinds of brows (and questions) to say, "I'm a Satanist" rather than some other anticipated response. It's unusual and unexpected. I gather most Satanists dig this too.

*7. A Sense of Purpose.* This isn't really unique to Satanism, but I do appreciate the fact that Satanism gives people a sense of meaning and provides something "worthwhile" to rally behind and support. All humans need something to believe in or we become apathetic and lethargic. Satanism lights a fire of passion and offers a sense of purpose.

## Criticisms of Satanism

*1. Satanism Is Reactionary.* The fact is, the best philosophies are developed out of the embrace of something positive, not out of reaction to something negative. But Satanism is overwhelmingly reactionary. The "reactionary factor" is evident even in the name of "Satanism." Satanism is a reaction to the hypocritical, stupid, tired, weak, boring failings of mainstream philosophies and religions. Rather than developing concepts intrinsic to itself, Satanism gathers its strength and power by feeding off of the weaknesses and failings of other systems of thought. The great pitfall with this is that Satanism can only be as strong as that which it reacts to. Like the Radical Protestants whose power and persuasion relied solely on the evils of Roman Catholicism and later died when the Roman Catholics got their act together, Satanism depends on the ignorance and stupidity of modern Christianity and other white light religions.

If you don't think Satanism is reactionary, just read a few Satanists' websites. Many of the authors sound like enraged frustrated teenagers who need a target to pin their angst on and need one now. Satanism provides them an outlet. There are exceptions to this rule, but this is the general attitude I've observed.

*2. Satanism Is Mainly Rhetoric.* Related to Satanism being reactionary, Satanism is "philosophy light" and "rhetoric heavy." Anton LaVey's greatest skill was that of a rhetorician. Satanism, if one scratches much beyond the surface, proves to be intellectually shallow. There's just not a lot to it. My gut reaction to the SB was, "It's Dale Carnegie's *How to Win Friends and Influence People* with an 'evil' twist and a large dose of [German philosopher] Friedrich Nietzsche thrown in. Satanism gets people motivated, excited, and impassioned—like all good rhetoric. But in the end, it's not intellectually satisfying as a philosophy in its own right.

*3. Satanism Is Too Dependent on Emotion and Human Ego.* Just like Satanism's forerunners, existentialism and gnosticism, Satanism's main target is the human ego. Most people are drawn and remain committed to Satanism because it feeds their ego. If you're told that you're special or elite or some other warm fuzzy idea when you embrace a philosophy, then you're more apt to buy into it and be blind to its shortcomings. Satanists thrive on the idea that they're somehow "the few, the brave, and the proud." In fact, Satanism uses the same rhetoric that the US military and religious cults use to win and keep the loyalty of their followers. If your ego needs to be flattered and this need is met in Satanism, then your ability to be rational and have intellectual clarity has been short-circuited on some level. This is the problem with all "feel-good" philosophies and religions. Like a habit one can't give up, people become dependent on the stroking of their ego and critical thought is sacrificed.

*4. Satanism Misunderstands Independence.* People need people. Many of us wish it weren't so because people have let us down, but the fact is, no man is an island. Satanists' claim of godhood denies this fact which is fundamental and necessary to humanity. This is one area where Satanists seem unable to face reality effectively. While individuals do in fact have much more power and potential than most ever acknowledge or realize, no one is independently good or independently powerful. In fact, you can only attain power if people give it to you. And when I say people need people, I don't just mean in terms of their usefulness, I mean people need the support and care of others. Babies will die if they receive no loving affection, and adults are no different. We all depend on others if we are going to be healthy and productive. Making independent claims of divinity, while it feels good, feeds one's ego, and has some self-empowering results, leads to a denial of that reality. And denying reality is always a pitfall; those that consistently deny reality will eventually find themselves powerless.

*5. Satan Is an Unworthy Symbol.* When Satanism was developed in the 1950's and 1960's in "Christian America," calling it Satanism had more power and punch because people's image of Satan was more heterogeneous, ridiculous, and stereotypical. Post the 1960's hippie movement however, people are more clued in to what Satanists are saying and the title no longer carries the same impact on people (with the possible exception of Christian fundamentalists). That which is based on shock eventually becomes mundane. The [Satanist] Black Mass, for example, has become expected and uninteresting—no longer the subject of newspaper articles or "scandal." Once again we see that Satanism, by being a purely reactionary philosophy, is dependent on the weaknesses of other systems of thought, or, in the case of the name, on the ridiculous stereotypes people hold of Satan.

And here is where I hold sympathies for Satanists. When "Satan" no longer shocks, one of the most "interesting" aspects of Satanism is lost. Satanism actually needs to grow into larger boots. I think if Anton LaVey were alive today he'd realize his short-sightedness. Satanism needs to have the flexibility to change with the times. As our world grows more and more secular, Satanists will be left holding yet one more tired, reactionary philosophy.

I would add that "Satan" has already been given a thorough definition by the world which is not entirely in accord with the Satanist's definition of Satan. Rather than merely redefining and re-creating a "Satan" to one's own liking as LaVey did, a more appropriate symbol should be chosen. Simple! Obvious!

**6. Satanism Depends on False Caricatures of Religion.** One of my continual complaints against LaVey and Satanists is that they thrive and make Satanism appear superior to all religions by simply mischaracterizing religious traditions through deliberate false descriptions and caricatures. One tactic often employed is simply to take the mistakes or radical extremes of religion that religious traditions have already *denounced* and hold those up as the "true" description of such traditions. What fool(s) would follow an anti-human, hypocritical, self-hating path? And yet, according to Satanism, all religious traditions that have flourished throughout the millennia have nothing more to offer than such folly. LaVey wrote, "Most traditional religions have little or nothing to do with reality, are dependent on obfuscation, interpretation, guilt, and unreasoning faith—some more than others." Aren't we lucky we have the "enlightened" Satanists to tell us the way it really is?

*7. Satanism's Self-Delusions.* By setting itself over and above all religious thought, Satanism claims to be the pinnacle of thought that sees through all the "mistakes" of religion and offers the corrective. It ignores and eschews the wisdom of the religious sages and prophets of the ages in favor of its own 20th century philosophical underpinnings. Like all fundamentalist and extremist groups, Satanism claims to consist of the elite who alone have attained an "enlightenment" in contrast to the "blind and dumb" masses who surround them. Satanists claim to be gods, to be "their own God." Essentially, Satanists have a superiority complex. One Satanist named "Warlock" wrote, "The point is, Satanists are superior. We deserve the best. Period. . . . We need to create an elite utopian community, and weed out all of the worthless slobs who dare try to be one of our kind. Destroy them all, and we will have a world full of Pretty Satanists."

Such an elitist position (for any group) requires an amazing amount of self-deception, delusion, deliberate misunderstanding, and the perpetuation of such misunderstanding among its proponents. Upon reading Satanist propaganda it is clear just how far such delusions will go: "I am a Satanist! Bow down, for I am the highest embodiment of Human life!" (LaVey).

Sorry Anton, but I'm not buying what you're selling.

# 10

# Counselors Can Help Students Reject Satanic Cults

*Lee J. Richmond*

*Lee J. Richmond is a licensed psychologist and professor of education at Loyola College in Baltimore, Maryland.*

*Cults, including satanic groups, generally attract alienated adolescents who seek a sense of belonging or a meaningful cause. But many of these groups engage in harmful activities. For that reason school counselors should do what they can to prevent youngsters from joining satanic cults as well as help youths who have already become involved in satanic cults. There are many actions that school counselors can take to accomplish these goals.*

The adolescents that become involved in cults are looking for a place to fit in. Especially appealing are the groups that offer an idealistic impact on the world. Although they promise structure, solidarity, and sometimes salvation, they are rarely truly altruistic. They cajole, manipulate, and eventually wrest wealth and work from unsuspecting teens who may be simply seeking a sense of belonging.

The destructive cults of which [school] counselors should be especially aware are: (1) Satanic groups, (2) groups that practice witchcraft and are attached to Satanism, and (3) neo-Nazi groups. All of these groups engage in practices that are very hurtful to others, and each of them engage in ritualistic practices. Each utilizes ritualistic symbols that are easily recognized.

Lee J. Richmond, "When Spirituality Goes Awry: Students in Cults," *Professional School Counseling*, vol. 7, no. 5, June 2004, p. 367. Copyright 2004 American School Counselor Association. Reproduced by permission.

## Satanism and Crime

Satanism is on the rise in the United States. It is a recognized religion and is therefore protected by the U.S. Constitution. By and large, Satanism is the worship of the devil as a deity. Many people who practice the faith commit crimes in order to achieve what they consider to be supernatural experience. Those crimes include torture and murder. [Cult expert D.H.] Thompson stated that according to police reports, "ritual killings, ritual abuse, grave robbing, animal sacrifice and destruction of property" have occurred in every state, "all in the name of religion, Satanism."

---

*Satanists disregard or condemn much that mainstream society thinks is right and just.*

---

According to Thompson, some examples of destructive behavior taken from police reports are: (1) corpses stolen from graves in Indiana, (2) eyes taken from a teen stabbed to death in New York, (3) the mutilation of teens in Texas, and (4) a manual about telling teens how to dispose of parents and sacrifice the family dog in California. In the name of Satan, youth have been known to beat, stab, and otherwise mutilate the bodies of other teens.

## Satanism and Adolescent Followers

Adolescents recruited to Satanism often do not know of these practices at the outset. However, in general, they do know the heavy metal music enjoyed by Satanists and the signature black clothing and dangling silver jewelry that Satanists wear. Adolescents who are initially attracted to these things probably do not know that silver is an impure metal, worn instead of gold because gold is a pure metal. Nor do many teens know that Satanists disregard or condemn much that mainstream society thinks is right and just. Often teens who are attracted to Satanist groups are simply innocent students who think that they are playing a more adult game of Dungeons and Dragons or imitating a favorite recording star. Student members, called "starters" or "doubters," are taught to carry a black book in which they record what they are gradually taught and the symbols of their creed. In it one might find drawings of daggers, hex signs, swastikas, inverted crosses, and the number 666, a sign for Satan in the Bible. In their book will also be the names of people that they hate, are taught to hate, or are told should be dead. Often members of Satanist cults are encouraged to self-mutilate and/or maim others. Many practice black magic or witchcraft as sorcery. Often formulas for their occult practices are kept in their black book.

Moreover, Satanist cults are usually kept secret. Little is written about them. However, local police know a great deal about these things because the teens recruited by [Satanists] are frequently caught committing anti-social and often criminal acts. Interestingly, the young people are told that such acts are beneficial and, quite frequently, necessary for the good of some nefarious cause. Sacrifice of animals and human parts are practiced by some Satanist cults. According to Thompson, teens become very frightened when they first experience a sacrifice. However, if they are not caught and remain with the group, many will become desensitized to such activity.

---

*School counselors can do many positive things to help youngsters stay away from cults altogether.*

---

Groups that practice witchcraft can be destructive if they are attached to Satanism. Witchcraft is a belief system that can encompass a magical view of the world. In addition to nature worship, witchcraft may involve the telling of fortunes, reading of the future, divination and the casting of spells. The pentagram within a circle is a symbol frequently used in witch craft. An upside down pentagram is Satanic in nature, and witches who are also Satanists are commonly said to practice black magic. . . .

## The Role of School Counselors

School counselors can do many positive things to help young-sters stay away from cults altogether as well as assist those students who are already involved in cults, dabbling in cults, and those who have walked away from cultic involvement. School counselors can also aid the students' parents or caregivers. To do this one must first become knowledgeable about cults, and especially about those cults that exist in the community and in the surrounding areas. . . . There is a great deal of information on the Internet. Enter into search engines such words as teen cults, Satanism, witchcraft, and occult, and the number of emerging web sites will be exhaustive. The problem with using search engines is in knowing the relative value of the material that one is reading. For instance, the reader will find in some web sites positive propaganda put out by Anton LaVey and The Church of Satan as easily as one can locate articles on how to recognize and deal with Satanic messages and the challenge of cult practices. In short, a literate and critical reader is needed to discern factual information. The school librarian could be helpful as a resource person as well. . . .

The school counselor should be a keen observer of who is wearing black clothing and heavy silver chains. The clothing may mean nothing, but it is wise not to assume either way. Counselors should befriend that youngster. Talk to the student about the music that he or she enjoys, the type of electronic games he or she might play, the motion pictures that he or she watches and so on. In time, the counselor might notice that the student is carrying a black notebook. If trusted by the student, the school counselor might ask what the book contains and if he or she can look in it. The question must not be asked in an accusatory way, but in a way that shows genuine interest and respect. Remember that most youngsters who are recruited by cults seek fellowship and spiritual enlivening. Should the counselor see a pentagram, 666 or a swastika, gently ask about its meaning. The youngster may or may not know the meaning, but the counselor will learn how indoctrinated the student is by the student's response. Naturally, the idea is to help the student leave the cult, but do not expect that to happen overnight. Involving the youngster in school group activities may help. Individual and group counseling may help counteract the pressure that most probably will be exerted on the student by members of the cult that the student is leaving. . . .

School counselors know and understand young people, and they are often the first line of defense in the protection of those students who have been involved in the twisted spirituality that many cults offer to students. Leaving a cult often precipitates an emotional crisis. The student in the cult and the student who exits it may experience depression, anxiety, fear, anger, and confusion. Students who abandon the cults that they joined must be reintegrated into the same families that they left behind. Furthermore, spiritual stability needs to be established, and this sometimes means a return to the house of worship that one left behind or finding a new one. The good news is that the great majority of adolescents and young adults who have had encounters with cults recover. Helping students do so can be a great source of satisfaction for school counselors.

# 11

# The Psychology Behind Beliefs About Satanism Is Deluded

*Malcolm McGrath*

*Malcolm McGrath is a political philosopher at Oxford University in England.*

*During the Satanism scare in the 1980s, a wide range of behaviors were labeled as "Satanist." Some anti-Satanists claimed that a seemingly simple act such as listening to heavy metal rock music could start a person on a path that might ultimately lead to ritual satanic murder. This "slippery slope" theory of satanic behavior lacks any sociological or psychological basis; however, it does make sense as a manifestation of the demonic-world illusion—the fear that a world of demons exists and under some circumstances they can enter the human world.*

One of the most perplexing notions surrounding the Satanism scare of the 1980s was the character of the alleged Satanists. Perpetrators of the scare such as cult-cops, social workers, psychologists, and Christian fundamentalists used the label "Satanist" to refer to an immensely wide array of behaviors. At one end of the spectrum were teenage dabblers in heavy metal rock and fantasy games such as Dungeons and Dragons. At the other end of the spectrum was a secret international conspiracy of Satanists, involving hundreds of thousands if not millions of Americans who performed organized ritual murders of up to fifty thousand people a year. At this level the conspiracy is so powerful, in-

Malcolm McGrath, from *Demons of the Modern World*. Amherst, NY: Prometheus, 2002, pp. 241–43. Reproduced by permission of the publisher.

volving some of America's most prominent citizens, and so well organized that it is impossible to detect. Between these two extremes were two intermediate levels. One was the so-called self-styled satanic criminal, such as the [1985 California "Night Stalker"] serial killer Richard Ramirez. Often such criminals tried to use Satanism as means of claiming reduced responsibility in court when tried for bizarre and brutal crimes, or spouted satanic lore once they were celebrities on death row and had nothing to lose. The second level of satanic involvement was the openly organized satanic religions, such as Anton LaVey's Church of Satan.

## The Slippery Slope Theory

What is particularly perplexing about this wide array of purportedly satanic behaviors is not just that they are all lumped under a single heading, but that the advocates of the Satanism scare suggest that they all form part of a single continuum. As cult-cop Detective Garry Sworin noted:

> Participation . . . could mean starting out with just listening to some heavy metal rock music, starting to read Satanic bibles, starting to be involved in a ritual, Satanic ritual, and then gradually lead to bigger and so-called, in their perspective, better things. You generally will be involved in what they call a black mass. You'll then be taken in and initiated as one of their members and one of the cult people. . . .

> Very definitely that's what we're talking about here because of the fact that you're starting out—or they're starting out with something that's very, very minimum, very small, which is dabbling, putting markings up and drawings up. And then all of a sudden it starts to progress, and all the contributing factors that we listed all come together and finally something happens where we go from what we know, what we should do, to the other extreme of what they want us to know and they want us to do. And at that point we're lost. And that is the really sad part.

Advocates of the Satanism scare promoted a kind of psychological slippery slope theory of satanic involvement; begin with heavy metal games and fantasy role-playing, and eventually you will be drawn into a secret, international, baby-murdering cult.

---

*The slippery slope theory of satanic psychology makes no sense in terms of current psychology, sociology, or historical precedent.*

---

## Argument Against Slippery Slope Theory

However, as critics such as police specialist Robert D. Hicks have pointed out, such a continuum makes no psychological or sociological sense. All four levels describe distinct and unrelated types of behavior. What is the relationship, for example, between playing fantasy games and becoming a psychopathic murderer? Research has shown that becoming a psychopath is the result of an inability to form emotional bonds, often relating to early childhood abuse, including in many cases physical brain damage. What does this have to do with listening to Metallica?

Sociologists who have studied cults such as Anton LaVey's Church of Satan have suggested that it is a kind of New Age, countercultural, feel-good religion. It appeals to people looking for a group affiliation who don't fit in elsewhere. How would psychopaths, who tend to be loners and incapable of group affiliations, fit into such an organization?

Also it is hard to see how any of these character types could fit into an international secret conspiracy involving some of the most powerful people in America. For such an organization to exist and be entirely secret, it must combine rigid discipline and spectacular efficiency with startling brutality, in a way comparable perhaps only to Hitler's Death's Head divisions of the SS, that carried out his dirty work in

Eastern Europe behind the front lines. These divisions were operated on the basis of rigid hierarchies, total subordination to authority, unquestioning ideological loyalty, and absolute group affiliation. It is hard to see how disaffected teenagers, psychopaths, or New Agers could find a place in such organizations. Furthermore, trying to imagine how one individual could pass through all the stages in the continuum leaves one simply dumbfounded.

## Demonic-World Illusion and the Slippery Slope Theory

In short, the slippery slope theory of satanic psychology makes no sense in terms of current psychology, sociology, or historical precedent. Given the lack of internal coherence to the theory, Hicks has suggested that it has emerged "because it presents a tidy ribbon with which to wrap up a nice neat package." Yet I would suggest that there is actually an internal coherence to the slippery slope theory of satanic psychology. Its foundations, however, lie not in psychology or sociology, but in the demonic-world illusion.

If you took the second paragraph of Detective Gary Sworin's commentary above and inserted it into the text of any number of modern horror stories, including *Dr. Jekyll and Mr. Hyde* or the movie *The Shining*, it would, idiomatic differences aside, be indistinguishable from the general flow of the story. What Sworin is describing is the Pandora's box version of the modern horror story.

It is a version where the demons are in some way presumed to exist outside of the individual, but the door to the world of the demonic is somewhere in the back of the mind. In other words, there are real demons out there, and if you begin to dabble in contacting them, they will take over your mind and turn you into a murderous lunatic. In this sense, the character of Jack Torrance in *The Shining*, is perhaps a slightly better analogy than Mr. Hyde. The logic of Jack's slide

Satanism

from a harmless fantasy relationship with ghosts to becoming a murderous demon mirrors almost exactly the slippery slope from heavy metal to ritualistic murder purported by advocates of the Satanism scare. And . . . this parallel is neither a coincidence, nor the result of one copying the other. Instead, here, as with the windows on the world of demons, the perpetrators of the Satanism scare simply fell prey to the same demonic illusion.

# Organizations to Contact

**Church of Satan (CoS)**
PO Box 499, Radio City Station, New York, NY   10101-0499
e-mail: HPNadramia@churchofsatan.com
Web site: www.churchofsatan.com

Created in 1966 by Anton Szandor LaVey, the Church of Satan is the first religion ever to be committed to Satan. The church believes that the essence of man's authentic nature is that of a sensual animal that exists in a universe where Satan dominates. Satanists believe that they represent their own deities. The Church of Satan has published its teachings in books such as *The Satanic Bible, The Satanic Witch,* and *The Satanic Rituals.*

**Cult Awareness Network (CAN)**
Cult Awareness Network, Los Angeles, CA   90028
(800) 556-3055
e-mail: can@cultawarenessnetwork.org
Web site: www.cultawarenessnetwork.org

The Cult Awareness Network's main purpose is to advocate religious tolerance and the preservation of civil and religious rights. The network maintains a large reference database, conducts public conferences, and offers a national telephone hotline for people who fear that their loved ones are associated with suspicious religious organizations. CAN has published a paperback book titled *The Cult Around the Corner: A Handbook for Dealing with Other People's Religions.* The group has several essays and articles on its Web site.

**Harvest Warriors**
PO Box 65, Clinton, AR   72031
e-mail: warriors@artelco.com
Web site: www.harvestwarriors.com/index.htm

Led by Reverend Daniel Yoder and his wife Rebecca (Brown) Yoder, the Harvest Warriors is a Christian ministry dedicated to spreading the teachings of the Bible. The ministry is committed to liberating people from satanism and other occult belief systems. The Harvest Warrior Web site contains a monthly newsletter and the group's Statement of Faith.

**International Cultic Studies Association (ICSA)**
PO Box 2265, Bonita Springs, FL 34133
(239) 514-3081fax: (305) 393-8193
e-mail: mail@icsamail.com
Web site: www.csj.org

The ICSA is a foundation engaged in researching cults and educating people about their social and psychological influence. ICSA conducts conferences and workshops. It also provides a significant number of resources and publications, some of which can be found on its Web site. The ICSA also publishes the *Cultic Studies Review* journal.

**Misanthropic Luciferian Order (MLO)**
e-mail: azerate_218@hotmail.com
Web site: www.mlo-scandinavia.tk

MLO is an organization that studies and engages in satanic magic. The aim of the organization is to construct an amalgamation of the ancient dark traditions. The MLO has a "Satanic Creed" that is displayed on its Web site. One of the organization's publications is a book titled *Liber Azerate: The Book of Wrathful Chaos*.

**Ontario Consultants on Religious Tolerance (OCRT)**
Box 27026, Kingston, ON
K7M 8W5fax: (613) 547-9015
Web site: www.religioustolerance.org

The OCRT is a Web site committed to promoting the spirit of religious tolerance. The site, which is maintained by a five-member team, was formed in 1995 in order to challenge erroneous information disseminated about various religions. The OCRT provides a complete and objective description of the world's different faiths. The OCRT Web site maintains a database of more than three thousand essays on various religious topics.

### The Satanic Alliance (TSA)
e-mail: tsao_2002@hotmail.com
Web site: www.angelfire.com/retro/alliance

Created in 2002, the Satanic Alliance works to achieve the goals of social, political, and economic improvement for all despite religious or philosophical differences. Some of the aims of TSA involve fighting terrorism, reforming gun laws, and eliminating special interest groups. The majority of TSA's members are Satanists. TSA publishes a CD that contains information on the group itself. Its Web site also covers other relevant information about TSA.

### Satanic Kindred Organization (SKO)
e-mail: skocouncil@satanic-kindred.org
Web site: www.satanic-kindred.org

The SKO was formed as an organization dedicated to uniting Satanists and satanic organizations. SKO works to spread information about contemporary satanism. The group provides aid for the homeless and for abused women and children. The organization displays its writings and poems on its Web site.

### Temple of Set
PO Box 470307, San Francisco, CA   94147
e-mail: ed@xeper.org
Web site: www.xeper.org

As a group that worships Set, an ancient Egyptian deity, the Temple of Set promotes the development of the self and consciousness raising. A spinoff from Anton LaVey's Church of Satan, the Temple of Set makes available on its Web site several essays on its beliefs.

## Watchman Fellowship
913 Huffman Rd., Birmingham, AL   35215
(205) 833-2858fax: (205) 833-8699
Web site: www.watchman.org

The Watchman Fellowship is a Christian countercult ministry whose primary aims are to educate local communities about new religious movements such as cults, occult-linked organizations, and New Age groups. The fellowship is committed to defending its followers against deceit and to the Christian proselytizing of cults. It also studies allegations of suspicious cult activities and conducts counseling for former cult members. The Watchman Fellowship displays on its Web site numerous essays on its beliefs. It has also published several videos and books, along with its *Watchman Expositor* magazine.

# Bibliography

## Books

Patricia E. Adams    *Fiery Darts of the Assassin: Know the Nature of the Enemy Satan.* Blountville, TN: Shekinah, 2006.

Gavin Baddeley    *Lucifer Rising.* Canada: Pub Group West, 2006.

Michael Barkun    *A Culture of Conspiracy: Apocalyptic Visions in Contemporary America.* Berkeley: University of California Press, 2003.

Blanche Barton and Anton Szandor LaVey    *The Secret Life of a Satanist: The Authorized Biography of Anton LaVey.* Los Angeles: Feral House, 1992.

H.P. Blavatsky    *The Origin of the Satanic Myth.* Whitefish, MT: Kessinger, 2005.

E.M. Butler    *Magic and the Myth of Satanism.* Whitefish, MT: Kessinger, 2005.

Thomas F. Coakley    *Spiritism: The Modern Satanism.* Whitefish, MT: Kessinger, 2006.

Stanley Cohen    *Folk Devils and Moral Panics.* 3rd ed. New York: Routledge, 2002.

Derek H. Davis and Barry Hankins    *New Religious Movements and Religious Liberty in America.* 2nd ed. Baylor, TX: Baylor University Press, 2003.

Lorne L. Dawson   *Cults and New Religious Movements: A Reader.* Malden, MA: Blackwell, 2003.

David Frankfurter *Evil Incarnate: Rumors of Demonic Conspiracy and Satanic Abuse in History.* Princeton, NJ: Princeton University Press, 2006.

Ronald M. Holmes and Stephen T. Holmes   *Profiling Violent Crimes: An Investigative Tool.* 3rd ed. Thousand Oaks, CA: Sage, 2002.

Tony M. Kail   *Cop's Guide to Occult Investigations: Understanding Satanism, Santeria, Wicca, and Other Alternative Religions.* Boulder, CO: Paladin, 2003.

William H. Kennedy   *Lucifer's Lodge: Satanic Ritual Abuse in the Catholic Church.* Reviviscimus, 2004.

Anton LaVey   *The Satanic Bible.* New York: Avon, 1977.

Anton LaVey   *The Satanic Witch.* 2nd ed. Los Angeles: Feral House, 2003.

James R. Lewis and Jesper Aagaard Petersen, eds.   *The Encyclopedic Sourcebook of Satanism.* Amherst, NY: Prometheus, 2006.

James R. Lewis and Jesper Aagaard Petersen, eds.   *Satanism Today: An Encyclopedia of Religion, Folklore, and Popular Culture.* Santa Barbara, CA: ABC-CLIO, 2001.

Gareth J. Medway    *Lure of the Sinister: The Unnatural History of Satanism.* New York: New York University Press, 2001.

Michael Moynihan and Didrik Soderlind    *Lords of Chaos: The Bloody Rise of the Satanic Metal Underground.* Los Angeles: Feral House, 2003.

Gilbert Murray    *Satanism and the World Order.* Whitefish, MT: Kessinger, 2003.

Debbie Nathan and Michael R. Snedeker    *Satan's Silence: Ritual Abuse and the Making of a Modern American Witch Hunt.* New York: Authors Choice, 2001.

J.R. Noblitt and P.S. Perskin    *Cult and Ritual Abuse: Its History, Anthropology and Recent Discovery in Contemporary America.* New York: Praeger, 2000.

Corvis Nocturnum    *Embracing the Darkness: Understanding the Dark Subcultures.* Fort Wayne, IN: Dark Moon, 2005.

Lawrence Pazder and Michelle Smith    *Michelle Remembers.* New York: Congdon and Lattes, 1980.

Alan H. Peterson, ed.    *Signs and Symbols of Satan.* Edison, NJ: American Focus, 2004.

Thomas Robbins and Benjamin David Zablocki, eds.    *Misunderstanding Cults: Searching for Objectivity in a Controversial Field.* Toronto: University of Toronto Press, 2001.

| | |
|---|---|
| Thomas J. Rundquist | *Drugs, Sex in Religions: An Uncensored Bibliography.* 2nd ed. Big Rapids, MI: Nova Media, 2004. |
| Tsirk Susej | *The Demonic Bible.* La Vergne, TN: Lightning Source, 2005. |

## Periodicals

| | |
|---|---|
| James Beverley | "Responding to Satanism," *Faith Today,* November/December 2002. www.faithtoday.ca/ article_viewer.asp?Article_ID=56. |
| David Frankfurter | "Ritual as Accusation and Atrocity: Satanic Ritual Abuse, Gnostic Libertinism, and Primal Murders," *History of Religions,* vol. 40, no. 4, May 2001. |
| Andrew Gimson | "The Dangers of 'Satanic Optimism': Andrew Gimson Believes That Pessimists Have a Much Less Dangerous Approach to the Human Predicament than Optimists," *Spectator,* January 14, 2006. |
| Eric Holmberg | "Hell's Bells," *Forerunner.* www.forerunner.com/forerunner/ X0005_.html. |
| Marcia Ian | "The Unholy Family: From Satanism to the Chronos Complex," *Journal for the Psychoanalysis of Culture & Society,* vol. 5, no. 2, Fall 2000. |

Jim Kouri          "The Pamela Vitale Murder: Satanic
                   or Ritualistic Crime and Murder,"
                   *American Chronicle*, October 22,
                   2005. www.americanchronicle.com/
                   articles/
                   viewArticle.asp?articleID=3116.

James R. Lewis     "Diabolical Authority: Anton LaVey,
                   the Satanic Bible and the Satanist
                   'Tradition'" *Marburg Journal of Reli-
                   gion*, vol. 7, no. 1, September 2002.

James R. Lewis     "Who Serves Satan? A Demographic
                   and Ideological Profile," *Marburg
                   Journal of Religion*, vol. 6, no. 2, June
                   2001.

Tina S. Moon       "Satanism: A Brief Introduction for
                   Law Enforcement Officers," *Institute
                   for Criminal Justice Education*, Octo-
                   ber 27, 2001. www.icje.org/id119.htm.

Andrew O'Hehir     "How Satan Is Propping Up Bush's
                   War on Terror," *Salon.com*, January
                   17, 2004. http://dir.salon.com/story/
                   books/feature/2004/01/17/satan/
                   index.html.

Frater Osiris      "I Was a Teenage Satanist," *Hermetic
                   Library*, 2001. www.hermetic.com/
                   osiris/teenagesatanist.htm.

Dawn Perlmutter    "Typologies of Satanism," *Anthropoet-
                   ics—The Journal of Generative An-
                   thropology*, vol. 7, no. 2, Fall 2001/
                   Winter 2002.
                   www.anthropoetics.ucla.edu/ap0702/
                   skandalon.htm.

Benjamin Radford  "Scott Peterson Defense Suggests Satanists," *Skeptical Inquirer*, vol. 27, no.
6, November/December 2003

Diane Vera  "Why 'Satanic Ritual Crime' Doesn't
Make Sense Even from a Christian
Point of View," *Theistic Satanism*,
2004. www.angelfire.com/ny5/dvera/
popular/S-crime-vs-Xian-S.html.

Timothy J.  "Adolescent Satanism: An Intersub-
Zeddies  jective and Cultural Perspective,"
*Journal for the Psychoanalysis of Cul-
ture & Society*, vol. 5, no. 2, Fall
2000.

# Index

Abrams, Joe, 10
Allee, John, 14
animals, ritual abuse of, 14, 23, 43
Anti-Christ, 48–49
*Apologie of the Church of England, An* (Harding), 11
Argentina, 37
atheism, 11
Australia, 37

baby breeder claims, 14, 15, 30
back masking, 32
Barton, Blanche, 25
Battles, Mary, 20
Beast 666, the, 13
Beasts of Satan (rock band), 19
Bemporad, Jack, 26
Bernall, Cassic, 55–57
Bible, 52
black masses, 47, 65
Blavatsky, Helena, 13
blood, shedding of, 48–49
Book of Lucifer, 59
Book of Satan, 51–52
Burt, Roger, 25, 26

California
    missing women and children in, 18, 19, 20–21
    ritual abuse in, 23, 24
children
    attraction of Satanism to, 26
    missing, 20–21, 33
    ritual abuse of, 23–24, 37
        at daycare centers, 29
        number sacrificed annually, 14, 32–33
Christianity, 52
    *see also* fundamentalist Christians

Church of Satan
    history, 13–14, 42
    interest in, 35–36
    philosophical Satanism, 11–12
    tenets of, 7, 9, 39–40
Columbine High School, 55–57
conspiracy theories, 33–34, 74
constitutional protection, 68
counterculture movement (1960s), 7
Coven of Bel Fire, 40–41
covens
    are more pagan than satanic, 40–41
    attempts to leave, 23
    rituals of, 25
Crabtree, Vixen, 50
criminal acts. *See* satanic ritual abuse (SRA)
Crowley, Aleister, 13
cult cops, 31
cults, appeal of, 67–71
culture of death, 37

daycare centers, 29
Deinsen, D. Rebecca, 60
*Demons of the Modern World* (McGrath), 7
dissociative disorders, 30, 31–32
domestic terrorism, 46–47
Dorchas, 40
doubters, 69
drug parties, 48
Dungeons and Dragons, 16, 26

Eleven Satanic Rules of the Earth, 51
Elias, Thomas D., 22
elitism, 66
emotionalism, 63–64

evangelical Christians, *See* fundamentalist Christians
evidence of satanic ritual abuse
   exists, 19–20
     con, 8, 14, 16
     confessions as, 42–43
     recovered memory therapy and, 15
     financial motivations for, 30, 31
     media ignores, 18–19
     symbols, 22–23
*Exorcist, The* (movie), 42

false memories, 15, 30
financial motivations, 30, 31
Finland, 37
First Church of Satan, 11–12, 14
France, 13
freelance satanists, 24, 25, 29
Freemasons, 13
*Frontline* (television program), 31–32
fundamentalist Christians
   definition of Satanism, 10
   former satanists as converts to, 30
   fuels satanic panic, 14
   rise of, 16
   Satanism is necessary for theology of, 25, 33–34

Garde, Mike, 41–42, 43
*Geraldo* (television program), 19, 28–29
Germany, 37
grave desecrations, 41
Greece, 37
Greek, Cecil E., 27

Haagen, Frank, 42
*Hammer of Witches, The* (Kramer and Sprenger), 12–13
Harding, Thomas, 11
heavy metal music, 19, 26, 68
Hermetic Order of the Golden Dawn, 13
Herzog, Albrecht Immanuel, 36
Hicks, Robert D., 31, 74, 75
honesty, 61
horror fiction, 75–76
Howell, Jim, 35
Hoyt, Karen, 24
human sacrifice, 14, 32–33, 37
hypocrisy in society, 61

independence
   Satanism misunderstands, 64
   Satanism promotes, 9, 41, 61, 62
individualism, Satanism promotes, 41, 42, 46, 61
indulgence, 7
*In Pursuit of Satan* (Hicks), 31
integrity, 9
Internet, 35–37, 47–48, 70
Italy, 19

Jack Torrance (fictional character), 75–76
John Paul II (pope), 37
Judaism, 52

King, Stephen, 75–76
Kramer, Heinrich, 12–13
Kranyak, Joseph, 24
Kuzina, Yelena, 37

LaVey, Anton, 7, 13, 24–25, 42, 65–66
lecturers, 31
Lévi, Eliphas, 13

Lucifer, 13
*Lure of the Sinister: The Unnatural History of Satanism* (Medway), 11

magic, 12–13
*Malleus Maleficarum* (Kramer and Sprenger), 12–13
materialism, 43
McGrath, Malcolm, 7, 72
media
    fuels satanic panic, 7–8, 14, 19, 28–29, 31–33
        con, 18–19, 44
    portrays Satanism accurately, 47
    portrays Satanism negatively, 42
    Religious Right characterization of popular, 16
Medway, Gareth J., 11
memory, 15, 20, 30
*Michelle Remembers* (Smith and Pazder), 7–8, 14
Miller, William Arthur, 20
moderation, Satanism opposes, 7
monotheism, 53
movies
    portrays Satanism accurately, 47
    portrays Satanism negatively, 42
    violence in, 16
music
    back masking, 32
    satanic, 19, 26, 68

Naglowska, Maria de, 13
Nathan, Debbie, 27, 28, 34
neopagan traditions, 10, 40–41, 42
Nine Satanic Statements, 7, 51
nonconformity, Satanism promotes, 9, 41, 42, 46, 61

occult, 40
Order of Nine Angels, 12, 13
Order of the Lion, The, 19–20
*Oxford English Dictionary* (OED), 11

pagan traditions, 10, 40–41, 42
Pazder, Lawrence, 7, 14
pentagrams, 22–23, 69–70
Peterson murder case, 18, 19, 20
philosophical Satanism, 11–12
police, 31, 33
Power, Ed, 39
psychiatrists, 31
punishment, revenge as, 53–54
pure knowledge, Satanism promotes, 7

Queen of the Apostles University, 35

Ramirez, Richard, 22, 73
Raphael, Sally Jesse, 28
reactionary factor, 62–63, 65
recovered memory therapy (RMT), 15, 20, 30
Regina Apostolorum University, 35
religion
    constitutional protection of, 68
    decline of, has left opening for Satanism, 42
    historically has led to violence, 53, 56
    satanic view of traditional, 65–66
    Satanism as symbol of resistance to traditional, 11–12
    Satanism rejects values of, 45
Religious Right. *See* fundamentalist Christians
religious Satanism, 12
repressed memories, 15, 30

revenge
    in Christianity and Judaism,
      52
    fosters self-preservation, 58
    is form of social justice, 52,
      53–54
    is justification for violence,
      25, 51
    Satanism promotes, 7
rhetoric, 63–64
Richmond, Lee J., 66
ritual slaughters, 23
Rivera, Geraldo, 19, 28–29
role-playing games, 16, 26
Roschke, Carl, 46–47
Ruda, Daniel, 42
Ruda, Manuela, 42–43
Russell, Jeffrey Burton, 12–13
Russia, 37

*Sally* (television program), 28
Santeria, 10
Satan, 40–41
*Satanic Bible, The* (LaVey), 13, 42
    promotes violence, 45, 46
    ritual abuse in, 24–25
satanic panic
    beginning of, 7–8
    causes of
      media, 7–8, 14, 19, 28–29,
        31–33
      psychological, 16, 72–76
    charges made during, 14
satanic ritual abuse (SRA), 8–9
    desensitization to, 69
    is result of freelance satanists,
      24, 25
    is worldwide, 37–38
    media reports of, 19, 28–29
    missing women and children
      and, 20–21
    police reports of, 68
    types of, 14

    of women and children, 14,
      23–24, 29, 32–33, 37
    *see also* evidence of satanic
      ritual abuse
Satanism
    definitions, 10–12, 40
    history, 12–14
    is form of fundamentalism,
      66
    negative aspects, 62–66
    positive aspects, 61–62
    as resistance to dominant
      religions, 11–12
    tenets of, 42, 53–55, 57–58
*Satan's Silence* (Nathan), 27, 28,
    34
Satan's Underground, 19
*Satan's Underground* (Stratford),
    14
school counselors, role of, 67,
    70–71
secrecy, 69
self-delusions of Satanism, 66
self-empowerment, Satanism pro-
    motes, 9, 54, 61
self-gratification, Satanism pro-
    motes, 39–40
self-hypocrisy, Satanism opposes,
    7
self-preservation, Satanism pro-
    motes, 57–58
self-styled satanists, 24, 25, 29
Sellers, Sean, 29–30
Set (Egyptian god), 12
sexual freedom, 42
*Shining, The* (King), 75–76
Shroder, Jen, 18
slippery slope theory, 73–76
Smith, Michelle, 7, 14
Snedeker, Michael R., 27, 28, 34
social justice, 52, 53–54
social paranoia, 16
*Social Psychology of Social Move-
    ments, The* (Toch), 33

Sprenger, Jacob, 12–13
starters, 69
Stratford, Lauren, 14
subliminal suggestion, 32
superior complex, 66
Sworin, Garry, 73, 75
symbols, 22–23, 64–65, 69–70

"Talk Back with Bob Larson"
  (radio program), 14
Tauzer, Stephen, 24
teenagers
  attraction of Satanism to, 8,
    25–26, 36–37, 67–71
  natural curiosity of, 41
  satanist, 29–30, 37–38
  web sites lure, 47–48
television
  cartoons, 32
  fuels satanic panic, 19, 28–29,
    31–32
  violence on, 16
Temple of Set, 11–12, 13
Texas, 19
theism, 12
Theosophical Society, 13
Thompson, D.H., 68
Toch, Hans, 33
Torah, 52

traditional Satanism, 12
turning the other cheek, Satanism
  opposes, 7

Vatican, 35
Victor, Jeffrey S., 16
violence
  is part of all life, 46, 50, 53
  in media, 16
  Satanism justifies, 7, 9, 25,
    51–52, 55–59
  Satanism promotes, 45, 46
  traditional religions promote,
    53, 56
vitality, Satanism promotes, 7
Vodum, 10

Warnke, Mike, 30
weakness, Satanism opposes, 7
web sites, 35–37, 47–48, 70
Wicca, 10
witchcraft, 12–13, 69–70
women
  dissociative disorders, 30,
    31–32
  missing, 20
  ritual abuse of, 37

Yahya, Harun, 44